The
Little Mac
Book

The Little Mac Book

Robin Williams

Peachpit Press
Berkeley, California

The Little Mac Book

Peachpit Press
1085 Keith Avenue
Berkeley, California 94708
415.527.8555

ISBN 0-938151-21-5

0 9 8 7 6 5 4 3 2

Printed and bound in the United States of America

To my mother, Patricia Williams,
who made it possible,
and to my father, Gerald Williams,
who would have been proud.

I must thank Brad Mager for insisting that—
as an instructor of graphic design—
I not be computer-illiterate, thus leading me
into the exciting new field of electronic design;
Alex Drake, for so patiently answering
my interminable questions over the past few years;
Marilyn Flowers, Shirley Davis, and particularly
Richard Abrahams and Roger Karraker,
for their warm support and encouragement;
all my students, for whom this was originally prepared;
and Beverly Scherf and Mary Boston,
for taking care of so many of the details of life.

Acknowledgments

"In this work, when it shall be found that much is omitted, let it not be forgotten that much likewise is performed."

—Dr. Samuel Johnson, upon completion of his dictionary
1755

CONTENTS

CHAPTER ONE

KS, MEGS, AND DISKS

People who've been working with the Mac for a while start tossing around jargon like, "It won't fit cuz it's a 900K document," or "My SE has 30 megs," and people who are not familiar with the Mac feel dumb because it all sounds so esoteric and we're sure we'll never be able to understand all this sophisticated computer stuff and besides we don't want to know all that technical stuff anyway we just want to learn how to run the darn thing. Well, as far as technical stuff goes, all most of us need to know is the machine is magic. Pure, simple, magic. Like an airplane.

Knowing the difference between a bit and a byte and a K and a meg, though, can help organize things in your brain a little bit so what you are working with will make more sense. This is how it goes:

Actually, the computer isn't that smart; it can only count to one. Remember in school when we learned the binary system, which we have now completely forgotten about, except that for some reason you could only count from zero to one and you had to use exponential notation? Well, Mac uses a binary system: it counts zero and one—zero means Off and one means On. See, it sends these little electronic messages, each a series of Off and On. And each one of those little messages is a **bit.**

Now, one little bit doesn't tell the computer a whole lot, so it strings together a bunch of bits to create a more important message: eight bits, such as **01000001,** makes one **byte.** As you can see in the column to the right, one byte of information is still rather limited—it takes a lot of bytes to create any sort of document.

So a bunch of bytes is grouped together and called a **kilobyte.** You would think that a kilobyte would be a thousand bytes, yes? No. Since the computer can only count to one, the closest it can get to 1000 in its binary system with exponential notation is 1024. But we generally round it off and say there's about 1000 bytes in a kilobyte. And kilobytes are the **K**s everyone talks about.

Technical Magic

Bits

0 1
Each one of these is one bit

Bytes

01000001
This byte represents the letter A

Kilobytes

Approximately 1000 Bytes equals 1 Kilobyte

How do Ks figure in real life? Kilobytes are what disk space and file/document size are measured in; the larger and more sophisticated the document or the software program, the greater the number of K it will occupy on the disk.

Floppy Disks

You've probably seen the nice little 3.5" **floppy disks** that the Mac uses. A disk stores the information for running the computer, for operating the programs, for saving the documents you create. Originally the Mac could only deal with a single-sided disk (one that took information on only one side of itself), but unless you have a very old machine with only a single-sided drive, you won't be using single-sided disks.

Disk Capacity

A double-sided disk can hold about **800K** (kilobytes) worth of data. Four pages of double-spaced typewritten text takes about 6K; therefore, you can get about *500 pages* of textual information on one disk (leaving some room for the messages it has to send to the computer). Spreadsheets, graphics, and other complex info take up a lot more space, of course.

Caring for Floppy Disks

Why is it called a floppy disk when it's not floppy? Actually, it is floppy. If you slide over that metal end you'll see the floppy disk inside. Don't touch it! It's full of tiny messages that your oily fingers or sharp nails can destroy. Keep your disks away from heat: they'll warp just like a record album when left in your hot car. And keep them away from magnets—a magnet will destroy all the data on the disk. So don't attach them to your refrigerator; don't store them near your telephone or stereo or any other electronic device; and don't pile them on top of your magnetic paperclip holder.

It is also recommended you don't keep disks in those little plastic bags they often come in; the plastic can build up static electricity which has the potential to destroy the precious data.

Initializing a New Disk

When you buy your floppy disks, they aren't *formatted* and so must be **initialized.** They come that way because other types of computers are now using these handy little things, and they can be initialized for either type. So when you first insert an uninitialized disk, Mac asks you several questions. You need to name the disk and you need to choose to initialize it single-sided or double-sided. Obviously, if it's a double-sided disk you'll choose double-sided. The system may warn you that you are going to erase all the information on the disk, but since it's blank, so what. When you finally click OK, Mac will lay down the formatting it needs to store all the valuable info you will be giving it.

It is possible to lock a disk. When a disk is **locked,** whoever is using it cannot change anything on it. Neither can it be printed from, nor can other files be saved onto it. To lock a disk, find the little black tab in the corner. You'll notice you can slide it up or down.

- When the tab covers the hole, the disk is unlocked.
- When you can see through the hole, the disk is locked.

A **hard disk** is actually a large, *hard disk*, rather than a floppy piece of film. In principle it works the same as a floppy disk, but it can hold a great deal more data. The hard disk itself can be installed inside your Mac, or it may be a separate unit. Either way, a hard disk is a storage container for holding all your documents and software applications, and typically holds your *System Folder* for starting your machine (see pages 9–11 for more info on the System Folder). Hard disks allow you to store your applications and documents all on one disk instead of on a lot of separate floppies, making it *much* easier and faster to work. It is essential now to have a hard disk, as applications and documents are rapidly outgrowing even the double-sided disks.

In fact, a hard disk holds so much data that it's not even measured in kilobytes; it's measured in **megabytes,** also known as **megs.** You've already figured out that one megabyte is 1024 kilobytes, right? Right.

Now, 1024 kilobytes (one megabyte) is more than what *one* floppy disk can hold. Hard disks come in various sizes, able to store from 20 megs to 30 to 40 to 60 to 80 megs of information, and they're getting bigger all the time. So on a small hard disk then, say 20 megs, you have as much storage space as on *more than 25 floppy disks!* You can load all kinds of applications onto your hard disk and create all kinds of documents without having to fiddle

Locking a Disk

This disk is unlocked

Hard Disks

Megabytes

Approximately 1000 K equals one Megabyte

with putting floppies in and out. As the software applications get more and more sophisticated, they take up more and more space, and already there are applications that just can't be used without a hard disk.

Backup Disks

Always **backup** your software applications. As soon as you buy a new application, make a copy of all the disks and **use the copy;** keep the originals safe in a clean, dust-free place. That way if a catastrophe happens to befall your application that you paid so much money for, you always have an extra copy. Software companies won't give you a new copy if you destroy yours. Funny.

Also always make sure you have a current backup copy of *everything* on your hard disk—all your documents you have so laboriously created. A hard disk can "crash" and leave no survivors. At the end of each working day, or more often if it is really important, make copies (page 35) onto disks of everything you created or modified that day (label the disks!).

You certainly don't want to completely lose all that data. A hard disk comes with a back-up application—be sure to check it out. If you are in a situation where there are massive amounts of information to backup regularly, check into the systems designed specifically for the process.

Rule Number 3

Back Up Often. Like everday.

(No, you didn't miss Rules 1 and 2—Rule 1 is on page 63; Rule 2 is on page 42.)

CHAPTER TWO

STARTING UP

The Mac turns on with a little switch on the back left of the machine—admittedly a very inconvenient place. A Mac II, though, can also be turned on with either the big key with the triangle on it at the top of the SE keyboard (that key that is useless for everybody else), or the key on the top far right on the extended keyboard. It's recommended on a Mac II that you always use the keyboard for turning it on and off, rather than the switch on the back.

Turning It On

If you have an *internal hard disk* for your machine, as soon as you turn it on it will **boot up** from the System on the hard disk. (The term "boot up" comes from the idea of pulling itself up by its bootstraps, as the Mac is going into its own System and turning itself on.)

Internal Hard Disk

If you have an *external hard disk*, that piece of hardware should be turned on first, and then turn on your Mac.

External Hard disk

If your computer has *any other switches* for turning it on, either on top of the monitor or on the keyboard, the switch on the back of the Macintosh must always be turned on as well (see page 91).

Other Switches

If you don't have a hard disk (you can read a little about hard disks on page 7), then you must insert a floppy disk with a **System Folder** on it. The System Folder, whether it is installed on your hard disk or stored on a floppy, must have at least two icons in it: the System icon and the Finder icon. Without those two items in the machine, it can't start itself up; it will spit out any other disks you try to insert and will give you the sad-Mac face. In fact, if those two icons are inside a folder, the folder must be named *System Folder* or Mac can't find them.

System Folder

System Folder

The **System** and the **Finder** are sort of like this: You are going on a trip. Your car is full of gas. You have the keys. You put a key in the ignition and start the car; the engine hums. But you can't get to where you're going yet—your car will sit in the driveway all day humming away until what? (Go ahead—think a minute.) Until you *put it in gear.* And that's sort of like what the Mac does: Your machine's plugged in. You turn it on. The screen gets

The System and The Finder

System

Finder

bright and that little picture is flashing. But you're not going to get anywhere until you *put it in gear* by inserting a System and a Finder (the Finder runs the Desktop).

Inserting a Disk

If you are not working from a hard disk, then the System disk is inserted into the **internal drive** (the *drive* is the little slot in the machine that takes the disk). Disks go in with the label-side up (the side that does *not* have the *round* metal piece on it), and the metal end goes in first. Your application, or program disk, then goes into the **external drive** (usually a little box that sits on the right side of the computer). You can save data onto either disk, provided there is enough room. (Some Macs have two drive slots on the monitor; in that case, put the System disk into the top slot and the application disk into the bottom one.)

If you're working from a hard disk, then your applications are probably already inside the computer and you won't need to insert any other disks to access them. You'll be inserting disks to save back-up copies or to install other files onto your hard disk. Either way, on the right side of the screen you will see icons, or pictures, of the start-up disk and any others that have been inserted (see Chapter 8 for more info on icons).

Whichever disk icon appears on your desktop in the upper right corner is the *start-up* disk, the disk that holds the System Folder the Mac was booted (started) with.

System and Software Versions

All computer software is constantly being upgraded and updated, making them more efficient, powerful, magical. The developers let you know which upgrade you have by labeling them with **version numbers.** At the moment of this going to press, the Macintosh System version is 6.04; the Finder version is 6.1.

As the Systems upgrade, the software programs are created to work with the particular nuances of the newer System, so it's a good idea to keep up on them. Although you don't *have* to use the newest System, it's free, so why not take advantage of it?

Only One System per Computer!

There should never be more than one System in the computer. Certain circumstances will cause the Mac to switch from one System to another, invariably ending in a bomb (see page 93).

CHAPTER THREE

THE DESKTOP

The Desktop or Finder

The **Desktop** is what you see on the screen when you first boot up your Macintosh; it's also known as the **Finder.** Consistent with the Mac environment that analogizes everything to parts of our real life, this Desktop works much the same as your desktop at home or in your office. You have desk accessories (under the Apple menu) such as a calculator, a clock, and a note pad; you have a filing cabinet (the disk) that stores all your file folders full of information; you have as many file folders as you could possibly want to organize it all; you can put folders inside of folders inside of folders *ad infinitum* (well, about 12 layers anyway) just like you would organize your hanging files. You even have a trash can.

It's a good idea to keep your Desktop organized, just like you would your office desktop. Create new folders (from the File menu; also see page 31) for each category of information, and store all applicable files in it. If you create a new folder at the Desktop before you begin work in an application, then you can put your new document right into that folder when you *Save* (see page 33)—that way, when you come back to the Desktop, everything is organized and in its folder so nothing gets misplaced.

Whenever you Quit working in an application, Mac automatically takes you back to the Desktop. If you don't see the name "Special" in the menu, or if there is no trash can, *you are not at the Desktop*—you are still in the application. To get to your Desktop, from the File menu choose "Quit," not "Close."

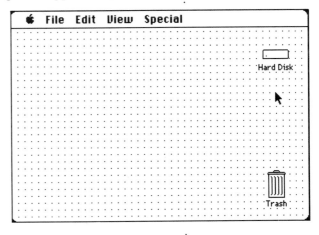

The Desktop;
also known as the Finder

Organizing Your Desktop

Below is an example of a **neatly organized Desktop** window, utilizing the *hierarchal filing system* (HFS), which is a fancy way of saying folders-inside-of-folders. Each category of software or documentation has its own place, and inside these folders may be other folders, each compartmentalizing specific data. It's much easier to keep things organized on a Macintosh Desktop than it is on an oak desktop.

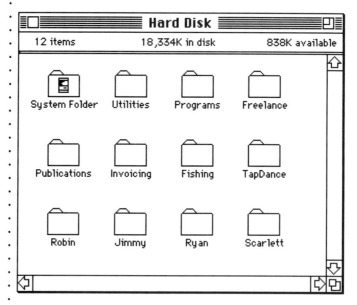

A hard disk window on the Desktop, using the folders to organize all the files

CHAPTER FOUR

THE MOUSE

The **mouse,** of course, is that handy little piece of hardware that controls the movement of the cursor on the screen. As you move the mouse across the desk, the cursor moves across the screen in the same direction. In most Macintosh applications, you cannot fully utilize the program without the mouse. A few programs give you the option of doing absolutely everything from the keyboard if you choose; but why learn 450 keyboard commands—isn't that exactly what we're trying to avoid?

The mouse is used in several different ways:

A **single-click** is a quick, light touch on the button of the mouse, with the cursor (be it a pointer or an I-beam or anything else) located at the spot of your choice on the screen.

> A single click with the arrow on an icon at your desktop will *select* the icon; a single-click of the I-beam will *set down an insertion point.*

A **double-click** is a quick click-click on the button, again with the cursor located at the appropriate spot on the screen. A double-click has to be quick and the mouse must be still, or it will be interpreted as two single clicks.

> Double-clicking on most files will *open* that file; double-clicking on a word will *select* that word for editing.

A **press** is simply pointing to something and *holding* the mouse button down.

> Pressing with the pointer on the *menu* lets you see the commands under that item; pressing on the arrows in a scroll bar *scrolls* through that window.

Press-and-drag is to point to the object or the area of your choice, *hold/press the mouse button down,* and *drag* across, letting go when you reach your goal.

> *Choosing menu commands* is a press-and-drag function; *dragging icons* across the screen is a press-and-drag function; *selecting text* is a press-and-drag function.

The Mouse

Single Click

Double Click

Press

Press-and-Drag
(also known, misleadingly, as click-and-drag)

The Pointer   When you're using the pointer, remember that the part of the pointer that does the trick is the *very* tip, called the "hot spot." So be sure that the extreme point is in the area you want to do something to.

The hot spot . . . .

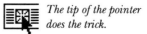

The tip of the pointer does the trick.

Cleaning the Mouse   It's important and easy to keep your mouse clean. As you're rolling it around you can feel if any cat hairs or dustballs have gotten inside. Take it apart regularly and clean it, following these steps:

1. Take the mouse in your hand and turn it upside-down.

2. With your thumbs, slide the round wheel to the left until the little marker on the wheel points straight up to the "O" (those little symbols on the back of the mouse actually are an "O" and an "L" for Open and Lock). This will open the lid.

3. Turn it back over into your left hand so the lid and the ball fall out into your palm.

4. You can clean the ball with a soft, dry cloth; clean the rollers inside with a cotton swab dipped in rubbing alcohol.

5. When clean, put the ball in your left hand; with your right hand place the mouse on top of the ball and flop your hands over. This places the ball safely into its little cubby.

6. Put the lid back on and twist it to the right, lining up the marker with the "L" for Lock.

7. That's it!

CHAPTER FIVE

THE MENU

Across the top of the screen is the **menu.** This is called a **pull-down menu,** because when you point to a menu item and *press* the mouse button down, a list of menu commands drops down.

🍎	File	Edit	View	Special

The Desktop Menu

To **choose** an item in the menu, simply keep the mouse button pressed and slide the pointer down; you'll notice that certain commands become highlighted, or *selected,* as you pass over them. When the command you want is highlighted, *just let go of the mouse button—don't click!*

Choosing a Menu Item

In some programs the pull-down menu itself contains a **pop-out menu** where you not only slide *down,* but also *out to the side,* usually in the direction of the arrow.

Pop-Out Menus

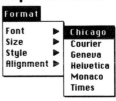

In the list, you can see that some **commands** are in **black** letters and some commands are in **grey.** When a command is grey, it means that particular item is not available at that moment.

Grey vs. Black Commands

The most common reason for it not to be available is that something was not *selected* before going to the menu; for instance, you cannot choose "Open" from the File menu if a disk or file hasn't been selected to be the one to be opened (to select something, click *once* on it).

15

Keyboard Command Shortcuts

To the right of the commands in the pull-down menu you often see a little code, such as ⌘N. This is a keyboard shortcut you can use *instead* of using the menu. If you hold down the Command key (the one with the cloverleaf symbol on it: ⌘) and press the letter associated with it, then the computer reacts just as if you had chosen that command from the menu. For instance, at the desktop pressing ⌘N will give you a New Folder in the active window (page 19), just as if you had chosen that item from the menu with the mouse.

The people who designed the Mac interface have been very thoughtful—as many as possible of the keyboard shortcuts are alliterative: ⌘**O O**pens files; ⌘**P P**rints; ⌘**E E**jects; ⌘**W** closes **W**indows; etc. Also see the following chapter.

Ellipses... & Dialog Boxes

Anytime you see an **ellipsis** (the three dots: **...**) after a menu command (as in "Open…"), it means you will get a **dialog box.** There are different varieties of dialog boxes, such as alert boxes or message boxes, but basically they all are meant to communicate with you.

Dialog boxes always give you an option to Cancel, so it is quite safe to go exploring menu commands this way. Just choose a command, check it out, then click Cancel. Even if you clicked around on buttons or typed in the dialog box, clicking Cancel will make sure none of your changes are put into effect.

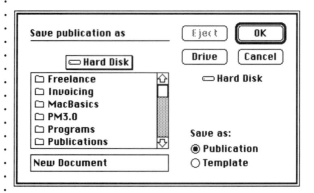

A "Save as…" dialog box; notice you can Cancel. You could also choose to eject a floppy disk before you Cancel if you need to swap disks.

CHAPTER SIX

IMPORTANT KEYS

There are several keys on the Macintosh **keyboard** that are particularly important and useful. They come in handy for shortcuts, manipulating images, accessing alternate characters, and any number of things in specific applications.

Speaking of keyboards, there are basically three kinds for the Mac: the two *standard* keyboards with the keypad at the end (like a ten-key adding machine)—one version for the Mac Plus and one for the SE—and the *extended* keyboard that has all the function keys and other little arcane sets of keys. Often people think the *standard* keyboard is the *extended* one because it has the keypad that we didn't have on our typewriters. It isn't. Both the Mac Plus and the SE generally have standard keyboards, but there are several keys that are placed differently, depending on which model (SE or Plus) you have. No matter where they are placed, though, they all have the following keys.

The symbol noted under each heading is the symbol that appears in menus to indicate pressing that key. They are usually used in combination with letters—always hold down all the descriptor keys (Command, Shift, etc.) and give a quick tap on the letter key associated with it. For instance, to Open files the command is often "⌘-**O**": hold down the Command key while typing a quick O.

The **Command key** is on the bottom row, the key with the California freeway cloverleaf symbol on it: ⌘ . On the SE and extended keyboards it also has an apple on it, and you may hear it referred to as the "Apple key." The symbols you see in the menu are referring to this key, and most applications have keyboard shortcuts utilizing it.

Next to the Command Key is the **Option key.** It's often used in combination with the Command key and/or the Shift key. It's through the Option key that you access the special characters, such as ¢ and ®, as well as accent marks, as in résumé and piñata (see page 46–49).

The **Backspace key,** called **Delete** on the SE and the extended keyboards, is located on the upper right. The name was changed to Delete because that's basically

The Keyboard

Command Key
⌘

Option Key

Backspace *or* Delete Key

what it does—whatever is *selected* will be removed when the Delete key is hit; whatever letter is to the *left* of the insertion point will be deleted as it is backspaced over.

Tilde Key
~
Escape Key
esc

The **Tilde key** (~) is located on the upper left on the Plus keyboard, and next to the Spacebar on the SE and extended keyboards. It's often called the Undo Key, because in certain applications it will undo the action immediately preceding. Although on the SE and the extended keyboards the upper left key now says **esc** (*escape*) and the Tilde has been placed next to the Spacebar, in many applications *esc* can still be considered the Undo key because it often does the same thing.

Control Key

The **Control key,** found only on the SE and Mac II key-boards, doesn't do much yet; in most applications it's just a dead key. They say it's something we'll grow into. You *can* type the Command key symbol with it: in the Chicago font Control–Q will produce ⌘.

Return Key

The **Return key** is often used for other procedures than simply starting a new paragraph. For instance, any button in any dialog box that has the double border around it can be activated with the Return key instead of the mouse. Different programs utilize it in different ways.

Enter Key

The **Enter key** on the keypad will also activate buttons with the double border, just the same as the Return key as noted above. Again, different programs utilize the Enter key in different ways.

Spacebar

The **Spacebar** is represented in menus by either the symbol shown to the left, *or as a blank space*. That'll really throw you. How long does it take to figure out that ⇧⌘␣ means press the Shift key, the Command key, and the Spacebar?

Shift Key

The Shift key is one of the most common keys used in keyboard shortcuts, symbolized by an up arrow.

Caps Lock

Just a note: the Caps Lock Key does *not* act just like the shift lock on a typewriter—in Caps Lock you get capital letters, yes, but you do *not* get the characters above the numbers or above the punctuation. If you want the shift-characters you must still press the Shift key to get them. Some keyboard shortcuts will not work if the Caps Lock key is down, so check for that if you're having problems.

CHAPTER SEVEN

WINDOWS

A **window,** as shown below, is a basic, fundamental interface of the Macintosh. If you conceptualize your disk as a filing cabinet in which you store all your work in manila folders, then opening windows is like opening file drawers to see what's in the cabinet. It's important to know all the little tricks in using a window, as you'll find windows in almost every application. They're simple.

· **Windows**

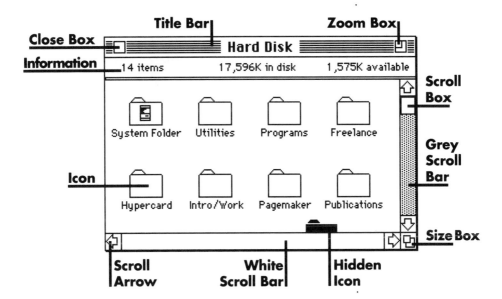

The **title bar** is the area at the top of the window in which, logically, the title appears. This title refers to the disk, folder, or document you have opened. If you press-and-drag in the title bar, you can **move** the window around the Desktop; it moves as an outline. Just let go when you have the outline placed where you want.

· **Title Bar**

· *Moving the*
· *Window*

If you have more than one window open, only one will have lines in its title bar; this means it's the **active window.** If the windows are overlapping, the active window is the one that is foremost.

· **Active Window**

The active window is the window that the commands from the keyboard or the menu will affect; for instance, if you go to the File menu and chose "Close," it will close the active window. If you ask for a "New Folder," the new folder will appear in the active window.

To Make the Window Active

To make a window **active,** simply click on any visible part of it; this will also bring that window to the front of any others. You may have to move other windows around in order to see the window you want to make active.

 To move a window *without* making it active, hold down the Command key while you press-and-drag in its title bar.

Grey Icons

 Sometimes you can't see the window itself but you *can* see the **grey icon;** in that case, double-click on the grey icon to bring its window forward and thus make it active. (Also see pages 27 and 73 regarding grey icons.)

Size Box

 On the bottom right corner is the **size box.** If you press-and-drag in the size box, you will make the window larger or smaller.

Zoom Box

On the upper right corner is the **zoom box.** If you click in the zoom box it will enlarge to fill almost the entire Desktop. If you click in it when it's large, the window will zoom back down to the size it was *just before* you zoomed it larger.

Scroll Bars

Along the right and bottom edges of the window are the **scroll bars.** The scroll bars allow you to view everything in the window, even if it cannot all fit on the Desktop or if the window is sized too small. You'll notice in the example on page 21 that the scroll bar along the right side is grey, while the one on the bottom is white.

Grey Scroll Bar

 When a **scroll bar is grey,** it's indicating that there are other items in the window you can't see. In the example on the previous page, you can see a folder along the bottom edge that is barely visible, so the scroll bar is grey, telling you something more is beyond its borders.

White Scroll Bar

 When the **scroll bar is white,** it's indicating there is nothing more in the direction of the arrows (the horizontal direction in the diagram) than what you can see.

Scroll Arrows

 At either end of the scroll bars are the **scroll arrows.** When the scroll bar is *grey* you can press on a scroll arrow, making the contents of the window glide past you as the scenery outside a train window.

Notice the little **scroll box** in each scroll bar—as you press on the arrows, this box moves so you can see where you are in the window. When the box is all the way at one end, that's the end of the window.

Another thing the scroll box is useful for is this: if you press-and-drag the scroll box, you can move it to any position on the scroll bar, let go, and the window will immediately jump to that particular place rather than scrolling through everything. This is very handy inside an application where you have a long document and scrolling with the arrows would take too long. In some applications a number appears in the scroll box to indicate what page you're on.

There's yet another way to use the scroll bars: if you simply **click** the pointer in any *grey* area of the bar, the window will move up, down, or across, usually a full window view—what was at the bottom of the view will then be at the top or vice-versa.

Just under the title bar you'll find some very useful **information:** *if your window is showing icons,* you'll see how many items are in that window, how much space is being used up on the disk, and how much space is left on the disk. On a hard disk, the numbers are still referring to kilobytes, so just round it off to megs by referring to the number in the thousands place (e.g. 7,856 would be almost 8 megs). *If your window is not showing icons,* then the information bar indicates how your files are currently being organized (see "Viewing the Window," below).

And, of course, in the upper left is the **close box.** Clicking once in that little box will close the window for you, sending it back to the disk or folder it came from.

Macintosh always tries to allow things to happen in a way that you feel is most workable for *you.* The **view of the window** is another good instance—you can choose to see what's in your folder in a variety of ways, all appropriate for different purposes or styles.

These different views are found, of course, in the View menu when you're at your Desktop. When you choose one, the active window will appear in that choice (the active window, remember, is the one that has the lines in its title bar). The view will stay that way until you

Scroll Box

Clicking in the Scroll Bar

Information Bar

| 4 items | 596K in disk | 175K available |

Close Box

Viewing the Window

Name
📁 Children
📁 Freelance
📁 HC Book
📁 Hypercard
📁 Intro/Works
📁 Tap Dance
📁 Utilities

Notice the underline in the information bar indicating which view is being shown

change it. As you change the views, you'll notice the name of the view you have chosen is underlined in the window.

While viewing the files as text, you can still manipulate them just as if they were icons (i.e. pick them up and put them in the trash or in another folder, rename them, copy them, open them, etc.—see Chapter 8 on Icons).

View by Small Icon keeps that feeling of looking at pictures, if that's what you prefer, but the icons are tiny so you can fit more in the window. They're not in any specific order.

View by Icon is what you typically see—pictures representing the data. Visually-oriented people tend to prefer this style. Again, the files are in no specific order.

View by Name turns the icons into text for those who prefer looking at words rather than pictures. A tiny little icon is still present so you can see what sort of file it is. They're arranged in alphabetical order by the name of the file.

View by Date organizes the files in a text format, in chronological order backwards from the date they were last *modified*, not the date they were originally created. This is handy when you have, for instance, several budget documents and you want to see the most recent version.

View by Size organizes the files in text form in order of size, beginning with the largest. It tells you how many K (kilobytes) that particular file is taking up on your disk. This is handy if you need to remove something to make room; you can see which files to remove to clear enough space. Unfortunately, it won't show the size of folders; to find their size you need to select the folder and choose "Get Info" from the File menu (see page 29).

View by Kind organizes the files by whether it is an application, a document, or a folder. This is handy if you want to see a list of all your applications, or all the documents in your budget folder, etc.

> View by Kind is particularly useful for a folder that holds an application and all its accessories— dictionaries, tutorials, technical files, samples, etc. This view will always put the application itself at the *top* of the list so it's easy to find.

When you're viewing icons in your window, they often get all scrumbled up and look like a mess. To align them all nicely, simply choose **Clean Up Window** from the Special menu—all the icons will fly to the nearest little cubby available on the underlying invisible grid.

> When they fly to the nearest spot on the grid, though, there are often spaces left available where another icon could fit in. If you want them to all line up in rows, from left to right with no empty places, hold down the Option key when you choose "Clean Up Window."

If an icon is selected, then the menu will say "Clean Up Selection," in which case just that selected item will be straightened up. Older systems may just say, "Clean Up." It works the same.

This is the button all houses must have—the dishes jump onto their shelves, the laundry puts itself away in the drawers, and all the toys go back in the toybox!

To **close** all the windows that are open on your Desktop, hold down the Option key while clicking the active window's close box; they'll all go away one after another!

Close All the Windows

> If you have System 6.0 or higher, you'll notice in the File menu there is a keyboard command for closing the active window: Command-W. If you want to close all the windows at once, press Command-Option-W and *all* the windows will fly away home.
>
> *Note: This will not work if a Desk Accessory is the active window; nor will it work if the Caps Lock key is down.*

> Another fancy trick to close all the windows is to hold down the Option key when you choose "Quit" from any application. Keep holding the Option key down until you see your Desktop. When you arrive, there won't be a single window open. If you use this trick you can legitimately call yourself a Power User.

> Often the file you want to open is buried within several folders. Hold the Option key down while double-clicking to open those folders; when you return to the Desktop they will already be closed.

Print the Window on an ImageWriter

Occasionally you may have a need to **print** the information you find in a particular **window;** for instance, to make a list of all the documents that are on that floppy disk, or all the dated budget files that are in the Budget folder. *You can only do this on an ImageWriter, though.*

To print the info in the window:

- Turn on the ImageWriter, making sure the Select light is on.
- Make sure the window you want the data from is the active window (click on it).
- Hold down the Command and Shift keys and press 4 (**Command-Shift-4**); when the printer responds you can let go.

Print All the Windows on the Screen

The above procedure prints only the *visible* contents of the *active window;* if you want to **print everything on the screen,** the whole screen and nothing but the screen, then do the same as above but this time press the **Caps Lock** down before you press **Command-Shift-4.** This way you can print the contents of any and all open windows whose contents are displayed.

CHAPTER EIGHT

ICONS

Icons—the little pictures you see on the screen—are another intrinsic part of the Mac interface. Instead of having to type in a code to get into an application or document, you simply click on the icon representing it.

Icons

> A note about clicking on icons—if you're trying to select or open it, don't click on the *name,* or the icon thinks you want to change the name.

When you initially turn on your machine and get to the Desktop (as on page 11), you'll always see an icon of the **disk** you're using, whether it's a hard disk or a floppy (the hard disk icon may look different than this one shown, depending on where it is and what kind it is).

Disk Icons

Floppy disk

- Single-clicking on a disk icon will select it.
- Double-clicking will open it to show you a window holding all the files.

Hard disk

> *Note:* If a disk icon is grey, it is either already open (page 27) or has been left in RAM after being ejected (page 73).

Whenever you have a window open, most likely you'll see **folder icons.** They act just like folders in your filing cabinet. Be sure to read the following chapter on Folders, as they are an important organizational tool.

Folder Icons

- Single-clicking on a folder will select it.
- Double-clicking will open it to show you a window with all the files that are stored in that folder.

Inside the folder named System Folder are all the **system icons** that help run the Macintosh, as well as a variety of icons that are for extra or fancy options. The ones that look like little Macs are system icons that perform essential operations. You'll see one called System and one called Finder—if those two are not inside the System Folder, you won't even be able to use your machine.

System Icons

- Single-clicking on a system icon will select it.
- Double-clicking will give you a message telling you an application can't be found or that it is locked or in use. That's because system icons are just visual

representations of the data on your disk that makes them work—there's really nothing to look at besides the cute little icon.

Printer Icons

Also in your System Folder are **printer icons.** In order to print to any printer, you must first have the icon inside your System Folder. If it is not in the System Folder, then when you go to the Chooser (see page 79) to tell Mac which printer you want to use, there will be nothing to designate and you won't be able to print.

- Single-clicking on a printer icon will select it.
- Double-clicking will give you the same message as the one you get with the system icons, for the same reason.

Application or Software Icons

MS Works

MacPaint

The **application or software icons** are the fancy ones. These belong to the application, or the software program, itself. Each application has its own design, so they all look different, but what they have in common is that they all try to give some sort of visual clue as to what they do. For instance, in the icons to the left you can see that MacPaint is an art program; Microsoft Works combines word processing, database, spreadsheet, and telecommunications.

- Single-clicking on an application icon will select it.
- Double-clicking will either open up to a new, blank page within that program, or at least to a dialog box where you can choose to *create* a new, blank page.

Document Icons

Budget   Article

Peaches

Document icons represent documents, or files, you have created in any particular application. Whenever you are working in an application and you save your document with a title, a document icon is created for you on your Desktop.

Document icons almost always look like a piece of paper with the top right corner folded down, or perhaps a sheaf of papers or a stack of cards. Typically they have some resemblance to the application they were created in, as you can see by the Works and MacPaint icons on the left.

- Single-clicking on a document icon will select it.
- Double-clicking will usually open you up to the application it was created in, with that particular

document on the screen. (If you get an error message, check page 92, "Can't open a file.")

When an **icon is grey,** as the one on the right, that means it's *already open*. Maybe you don't see its window because it's hidden behind another open window, but you know it's open somewhere. (If a floppy disk icon is grey, but it is not in the machine, see page 73!)

- Single-clicking on an open icon will select it.
- Double-clicking will bring its window to the front as the active window.

Open (Grey) Icons

When an **icon is black,** like the one on the right, that means it is *selected*—it got selected by clicking once on it. Once an icon is selected, you can press-and-drag it somewhere; menu commands will affect it, such as Open or Put Away or Clean Up Selection; you can change its name by typing.

- Single-clicking is what selected this icon in the first place.
- Double-clicking a selected icon will open it just like any other icon.

Highlighted (Black) Icons

The **trash can icon** works just like the trash can in your yard—you put things in it you don't want anymore and the garbage collector comes and takes it away and you never see it again.

Trash Can Icon

To put something in the trash: Press-and-drag an icon over to it. *When the can becomes black,* let go and the icon will drop inside. If you find a bunch of garbage hanging around outside the can, it's because you didn't wait for the can to turn black—you just set it down next to it. Try again. The *tip of the pointer* must touch the can!

To remove something from the trash: If you double-click on the trash can you'll find that it opens up to a window, just like any other window. So if you decide you want that item you just threw away, you can go get it. Either press-and-drag the icon back to the disk/folder it came from; **or** click once on it to select it, then from the File menu choose "Put Away" and it will go right back where it came from. How does it know?

Don't count on anything staying in the trash very long, though! Read on…

You can empty the trash by going up to the Special menu and requesting "Empty Trash." Once you do that, it's gone forever. No amount of crying or pleading or screaming or kicking will bring it back. Believe me.

Now, you can empty the trash yourself, as noted above. But sometimes the garbage collector comes when you're not looking, so don't count on it staying there 'til you empty it. Whenever you eject a disk, copy a file, Shut Down, Restart, or turn off the computer, the trash gets emptied. Whenever you open an application, the trash gets emptied. Whenever the power goes out, even for a split second, the trash gets emptied. And if the Mac runs out of RAM (random access memory, where every-thing stays until it gets saved to a disk), Mac herself will empty the trash for you and take that memory space. So be careful.

Whenever anything Mac thinks is important has been put in the trash, such as an application or system icon, you'll get a dialog box asking if you really want to throw that away. That's nice.

If you don't want to see the warning dialog box, hold down the Option key while trashing the item.

Unfortunately, Mac doesn't think anything *you* have created is worth warning you about.

When trashing items to make more space on the disk, the trash must be emptied before the space will open up; watch the numbers in the information bar of the window when you empty the trash.

Screen Dump

Screen 0

Occasionally you will see or create an icon that is named Screen 0 or Screen 1, etc.; this is a **screen dump.** The screen dump holds a picture of the computer screen at the time you pressed the special key combination.

Whenever you press Command–Shift–3, a MacPaint screen dump, or screen shot, is created for you; an icon for the shot will appear in the window that contains the System Folder. You can open MacPaint, open this file (or use SuperPaint with the MacPaint button in the Open box chosen), and view/change the image just like you would any other paint image. Then paste it into another document.

For instance, all the images in this book were created using screen shots. With the image on the screen in its natural habitat, Command–Shift–3 was pressed. Then MacPaint was opened and the Screen 0 file was opened. Since the screen shot took a picture of the entire screen, all the excess stuff around the image had to be erased. It could then be changed, resized, rotated, flopped, etc. The images were put in the Scrapbook and later pasted onto these pages.

You can create up to 10 screen dumps, and they'll be labeled 0 to 9; you can create more, but you have to rename the others first.

Get Info is not an icon, but a menu item that can give you important information about any file represented by an icon on your Desktop, be it application, document, system, printer, or folder.

Get Info

Select an icon, any icon, by clicking once on it; then from the File menu choose "Get Info." You'll get a little information window that tells you interesting things about the file, such as how big it is, when it was made, which software program it was created in, which software version you have.

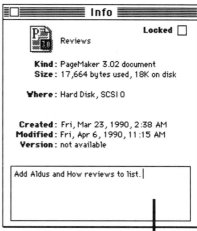

The nicest thing about this window is you can type in your own information in the box at the bottom (the insertion point flashes, waiting for you to type). This comes in very handy: you can write notes to yourself about that particular file and what it contains, briefly detail this budget file from that budget file, record any bugs you find in it, make note of further changes you want to employ, leave notes for your lover, etc. The information you type is automatically saved. (If at some point you chooose to rebuild your Desktop [see page 89], the rebuilding process will unfortunately destroy any Get Info notes. Darn it.)

This is the box in which you can type your own notes.

The info on the following page explains the little locked checkbox in the upper right.

Locking the File

Locked ☒

This file is now locked.

There is a **locked** checkbox in the upper right corner of the Get Info window. If this is checked (by clicking once on it), the file cannot be renamed or inadvertently thrown away—as soon as it hits the trash a dialog box will come up telling you a locked file cannot be thrown away.

It also becomes a *Read-Only* file—no one can save changes in it. This is handy for sending around copies of a document and ensuring no one accidentally changes anything. You can't even change the Get Info notes.

> ● If you hold down the Option key, you *can* throw away a locked file. Uh oh.

Locked ☐

This file is now unlocked.

To unlock it, simply click in the checkbox again. If there is no X, it is unlocked.

Moving Icons

To **move icons,** simply press-and-drag on them. You can put any icon into any folder icon, and drag them out of folder icons. Also see Chapter 10 on Copying/Selecting.

Renaming Icons

To **rename an icon,** click once on it. When it turns black, simply type and the name will be changed. If the name does not change, click once more on the icon; sometimes it insists on *two single clicks (not a double-click!)* as a safety feature protecting you from changing the name accidentally. Use standard word processing procedures to set an insertion point, double-click a *word* to select it, backspace to delete, etc., as detailed in Chapter 12.

Undo
Icon Name
Change

If you perchance do accidentally change the name of an icon (which is very easy to do—files have been known to mysteriously change their names to \\\\\\\\\\\ or `````` while you weren't doing anything but leaning on the keyboard), you do have one chance to restore it to its original form: Undo. As soon as you see this mistake has been made, from the File menu choose "Undo." *If you haven't done anything* since this minor catastophe (and things could be worse), Undo will restore the original name, even if you forgot it. If you are too late to catch Undo, you'll just have to rename it yourself.

CHAPTER NINE

FOLDERS

Folders are essential to the organization of your work on the Mac. They are, of course, visual representations of our office and home environment, and they function in much the same way.

You can consider your disk to be the main filing cabinet. When you store items in a filing cabinet, you don't just toss them in the drawer, do you? Can you imagine what a mess your filing cabinet would be without folders? Many Macintoshes become just as messy and just as difficult to find work in. It's very important to learn to take advantage of the folders.

You can **create your own** new, empty folders by choosing "New Folder" from the File menu, or by using the keyboard shortcut, Command–N. The new folder will appear in the *active* window.

The new folder shows up in the active window already highlighted, or selected (it's black), with the name "Empty Folder." Mac assumes you want to change the name, so while it is black you can just type the name you want it to have and the new name will appear. If you type an error, just backspace over it (use the Backspace or Delete key in the upper right of the keyboard) and continue typing. You can use up to 27 characters; you can't use a colon, nor can the name start with a period.

If you accidently unhighlighted the new folder before you changed its name, or if you want to change the name of any other folder, it is still very easy to do: simply click on the folder and it will turn black. You'll notice the pointer changes from an arrow to an I-beam when it's pointing to the *name* of the folder; this is a clue that whatever you type now will replace the title that is already there. So go ahead and type in the new name while it's black.

If typing while the folder is highlighted doesn't change its name, click once more on the folder; sometimes it insists on *two single clicks (not a double-click!)* as a safety feature protecting you from changing the name accidentally.

Folders

Creating a New Folder

Naming the New Folder

Changing the Name of a Folder

The pointer has changed to an I-beam

Putting Something Inside a Folder

To put something **inside** the folder, press-and-drag any icon over to it; when the folder turns black, let go and the icon will pop inside. The folder does not have to be open to place an item inside of it, and it can be grey. You can have folders inside of folders inside of folders, which is technically called the *Hierarchal File System* (HFS).

Opening a Folder

Double-clicking on any folder will **open** it to a window, showing you all the valuable information you have stored inside.

Removing Something From a Folder

To **remove** something, open the folder first, so you see its window and the icons inside, as below. Then simply press-and-drag the icon/s out, either to the Desktop or to another folder or window.

Note: Moving as opposed to Copying

If you are moving the icon to someplace else on the *same* disk, it will just pop out of that one folder and into the other. BUT if you are moving the item to a *different* disk, the original icon will stay put and a *copy* of it will be placed on the other disk.

Organizing Your Disk Using Folders

Below is an example of a well-organized hard disk; there isn't a bunch of junk lying around making it difficult to find things. (Would that houses were so easy to keep neat!) It's basically organized the same way a filing cabinet would be.

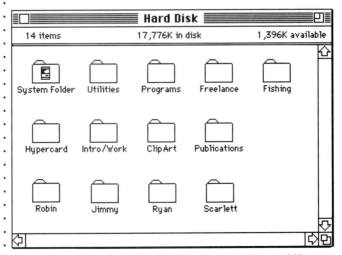

Everything on the disk (the "filing cabinet") is tucked into a folder; the folders may each have sub-folders to further organize their contents.

One of the best ways to keep windows tidy is to **create a specific new folder** for a new project *before* you create the documents for the project, and then *save the documents right into their own folder*. For instance, if you are about to create a budget report with seven variations, or a newsletter in which there will be ten to twelve separate stories, then follow these steps:

- **At your desktop,** *before* **you open the application** to start creating the reports, make your new folder and name it (let's name this one *BudgetNews*). This new folder can be inside of another folder, of course.

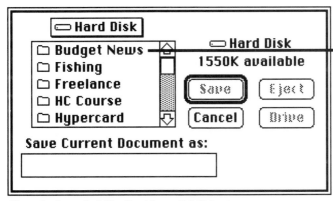

A new folder at the Desktop hard disk window, waiting for the new stories to be stored inside.

- Go into your application and create the first report.

- When you go to "Save As…" and name the story, find the folder *Budget News* in the Save As dialog box. You'll see the folder you created earlier listed here in the list box. Double-click on it to open the folder.

If you don't see the folder listed here, click Drive to see if it is on another disk. Or perhaps you have it tucked inside of another folder, in which case you will need to open that other folder first.

Creating Project-Specific Folders

In this example, here is the folder BudgetNews; double-click on it to open it.

• After you double-click on the name of the folder, you will see its name and an open folder icon in the label above the list box. If you choose to Save right now, it will be saved into *that* folder.

• When you go back to your Desktop everything will be right where it belongs, tucked into its own folder, and nothing will be forgotten or misplaced.

Make sure this label shows the name of your folder. If you see the name of your folder in the list box beneath it, double-click on that name to open the folder and make it appear here. When you save, it will always be saved into whatever folder or onto whatever disk appears in this label.

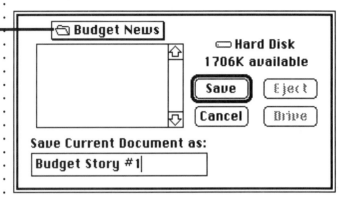

If you refuse to read and follow the directions and have lost files, do read about Mr. Find File on page 81. He'll go get them for you.

CHAPTER TEN

COPYING/ SELECTING

Copying files is an everyday task. You may need to copy an application from its original disk onto your hard disk; copy a report to give to a co-worker; copy a document to take to a service bureau for printing; create the ever-necessary backup copy; etc. etc. etc.

Why Copy?

Macintosh has made it as easy as can possibly be to **copy** files (which is why pirating, or copying software without paying for it, is such a problem for software producers).

Copying

> To copy, simply click on the icon representing the file you want to copy; then press-and-drag the icon to the icon of the disk you want to copy it onto. A little message comes up telling you it's being copied. That's it.

You may copy onto a disk, into a folder on another disk, or onto your hard drive. In every case, make sure that the icon of the place you are copying it *into* becomes *black*. When it is black, that means it's ready to accept the file/s. If it's not black, you'll just be placing it *next* to the icon, not *in* it. The *tip of the pointer* is what turns it black.

To **copy more than one** file at a time, *select* more than one file (detailed in the next paragraph); when more than one file is selected, dragging one file will drag them all together, either to the trash can, into another folder, onto another disk, or simply to clean up the joint.

Copying More Than One File at a Time

You may have noticed in a Desktop window that when you *press in an empty space and drag the pointer,* a dotted rectangle comes out of the tip—this is the **selection marquee,** common in many Mac programs. On the Desktop, any file that is even partially enclosed in this marquee will be selected.

Selecting More Than One File at a Time

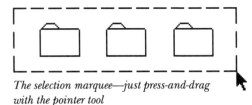

The selection marquee—just press-and-drag with the pointer tool

Selecting all the icons this way will of course turn them all black.

• When you press-and-drag on the *black* area of one of the selected items, they will all drag together.

• Clicking in any *white* space will *deselect* all the files.

Shift-Clicking to Select More Than One File

Another method of selecting more than one item is to **Shift-Click.** You may have noticed that once a file is selected, clicking on another file deselects the first one. *But,* if you hold down the Shift key while clicking, every one of the files you click will be selected. This way you can select several files in different corners of your window.

Shift-Click to Deselect

In the same manner, you can **deselect** one file at a time. For instance, if you group a bunch of files within the selection marquee but you don't want the one in the middle, simply hold down the Shift key and click once on that one—it will be the only one deselected.

Duplicate/Copy File on Same Disk

The Mac only makes a *copy* of a file if you drag the file to another *disk.* If you want to make a copy of the file on the *same* disk, click *once* on the file icon, then from the File menu choose "Duplicate" (or press Command–D). This creates a second version in the same folder named "Copy of ____." When duplicating or copying folders, every item contained within is also copied.

If you want to put a *copy of a file into another folder on the same disk,* a shortcut is to hold down the Option key while moving the file. (This does not rename the file "Copy of ____.")

Copy From Floppy to Floppy with Only One Floppy Drive

If you want to know how to copy from one floppy disk to another floppy disk when you have only one floppy drive, please see page 89.

CHAPTER ELEVEN

OPENING APPLICATIONS

Or Documents

The term **application** is often used synonomously with **program.** It refers to the software package you are using to create your documents, such as Claris MacPaint, Microsoft Works, Adobe Illustrator, etc. They all do something different; they all have a particular function. Sometimes it takes a little research to find the software applications to specifically meet your needs.

What is an Application?

To open an **application,** or software program, find its icon on the disk. Application icons, as noted in the chapter on icons, typically look fancier than anything else. Whether the program is installed on your hard disk or you are using a floppy disk, you will need to find its icon at the Desktop.

Opening an Application

MacPaint

Application icon

> From the Desktop, double-click on the application icon to open to a blank page, ready for you to create a new document.

> Some applications open to a commercial, or at least to an Open dialog box; in either case you can choose to create a new document at that point from the File menu.

To **open a document** that has already been created and saved in an application, find its icon on your Desktop.

Opening a Document from the Desktop

Peaches

Document icon

> Double-click on a document icon; most of the time this will open the application, placing your document on the screen as you last saved it.

A few programs won't allow you to open their documents from the Desktop. If the software program itself is *in* the computer, either on the hard disk or on a floppy, and you get the dialog box telling you an application can't be found, then you must *open the application first* and *then* open the document from the File menu by choosing "Open." See the section on the following page for maneuvering around the Open dialog box.

Now, just because you have an icon representing a document you created in a certain software application doesn't mean you can open up that document just anywhere. Double-clicking on a document icon will only

Important Note!

open it **IF** *the application itself is also in the computer,* either on the hard disk or on a floppy disk that is inserted into one of the drives. If the application isn't there, then the document doesn't have anywhere to put itself! (See page 93 for more info.)

New vs. Open · Once the application is up and running, in the File menu you see two choices: **New** and **Open.** This is confusing at first because one thinks, "Well, I want to *open* a *new* one." The difference is this:

- **New** creates a clean, blank page on which to begin to create a *new* document.

- **Open** takes you to a dialog box where you can choose to *open* a document that has been previously created and saved.

An "Open" · *This is the specific folder or*
Dialog Box · *disk the document is in. When*
the icon in the label here is a
folder, *this is a* **menu;** *press*
to see the hierarchy.
This is the name of the
disk you're looking at.

Folder names are black
(not grey) because there
may be a file inside that
you can open.

Single-click on
one of these names to
select *that file.*

Double-click the name
to **open** *the file.*

If it is a folder, as this
one is, it will open here in
this list box to show you
the files inside the folder;
if it is a document, it will
open that document
on your screen.

▭ **Hard Disk**

☐ **Fishing**
☐ **Freelance**
☐ **Hypercard**
☐ **Intro/Work**
☐ **Jimmy**
☐ **Newsletter/May**
☐ **Programs**
☐ **Publications**

▭ **Hard Disk**

[**Eject**]

[**Drive**]

[**Open**]

[**Cancel**]

Click **Eject** *to eject a disk so you can insert another.*

Click **Drive** *to see what's on the disk in the other drive.*

Click **Open** *to open the selected file;* **or** *you can double-click on the file name.*

Click **Cancel** *to take you back to wherever you were without opening anything.*

CHAPTER TWELVE

TYPING

Typing

In some applications **typing** is the main idea, as in a word processor. In some, it is the way to input the data whose purpose is to be manipulated, as in a database or a spreadsheet. In others, it is a sideline that is occasionally necessary, as in a paint program. And everywhere you find dialog boxes where you type in some answer or other, and even on your Desktop you can type in the names of files and folders. Fortunately, in the consistent Mac environment, every program reacts to typing in the same way.

The I-Beam

You may already be familiar with the Macintosh word processing **I-beam** (pronounced eye-beam): $\mathcal{I}$

In the Macintosh, the I-beam is a visual clue that you are now in a typing mode, as opposed to having an arrow or a cross-hair or any number of other cursors that appear in various programs.

> *The I-beam is simply another pointer.* And just like the pointer, it doesn't do anything until you *click* it.

The Insertion Point

When you move the I-beam pointer to a spot and click, it sets down a flashing **insertion point** that looks like this: | (but it flashes).

The Important Basics of Typing on the Mac

After you click the mouse and set the insertion point, then you can move the I-beam out of the way (using the mouse)—**the *insertion point* is what you need to begin typing.** With the insertion point flashing, anything you type will start there and move out to the right. This is true whether the insertion point is at the beginning or the end of a paragraph, in the middle of a word, in a field of a dialog box, under an icon at your Desktop, or anywhere else. (The only time the words will not move to the right is if the alignment has been set to align right or centered, or if a tab other than left-aligned has been set.) At any time you can take the mouse, move the I-beam pointer somewhere else, click it down, and start typing from the new insertion point.

Backspace/ Delete

Also from that insertion point, pressing the **backspace** key (found in the upper right, appropriately renamed the **delete** key on the newer keyboards) will backspace over and remove any letters in its path. So you can backspace/delete to correct typos as you go, or set the insertion point down anywhere else in your text and backspace/delete from there.

Highlighting Text

Highlighting text is a shortcut to backspacing over letters to remove them. All through the Mac environment, if you double-click with the I-beam on a word, the entire word is selected, indicated by the highlighting.

This word is highlighted.

If you want to select more than one word, press-and-drag over the entire area you wish to highlight.

Part of this line is highlighted.

What does highlighting do? Well, once a word is highlighted (selected), anything you type will *entirely replace* the highlighted text. Or you can now change the font (typeface) or style or size of the text using your menu commands. Or you can copy or cut or delete that text. Or you can paste something in to replace it. In fact, you *cannot* do any of these things *unless* the text is first highlighted. (Each of these procedures is explained in this chapter.)

To **unhighlight,** click once anywhere, even in the black space.

When to Use the Return Key

Word wrap: In a word processor, you *never* want to hit the Return key at the end of your line, *unless* it is the end of the paragraph or unless you *really do* want the line to always end there, as in an address. This is because word processors have *word wrap*—the words just wrap themselves around onto the next line when they get to the right margin. Why is that? Well...

Hard return: What happens when you press the Return key is that you insert what is called a *hard return.* Then if you were to change your margins, your line would *always* break at that hard return, even if there are only two words on the line. So, just keep those nimble fingers moving along and only hit the Return key when you want a new paragraph.

Double-space: Hitting the Return key twice is like pushing the carriage return on a typewriter twice—you get a double space between the lines. This is for extra space between paragraphs (although in most word processors you can ask for an automatic increase of space between paragraphs). If you want the entire document, or even just a piece of it, double-spaced—that's different; there is always an instant way to change your spacing to double-spaced. Check your manual for the method for your particular application.

Removing a return: The computer sees a Return as just another character, which means to remove a return you simply *backspace over it,* just like to remove an unwanted character. The problem is, in most programs you can't *see* the Return character. So you must set the insertion point just to the left of the first character on the line and backspace/delete, like so:

|here set the insertion point to *remove the empty line* above this one. Backspace/delete *again* to *wrap the sentence back up* to the one above.

The computer deals with **blank spaces** just as it deals with the characters you can see. Every tab, return, space-bar space, etc., is a character to Mac. This means you can select blank spaces, blank lines, blank tabbed spaces, or returns in order to delete them. Select and delete them just like you would any other character.

Blank Spaces

The space between
these ▮▮▮▮ words is highlighted.

In many applications
you can also select the blank space
▮▮▮▮▮▮▮▮▮▮▮▮▮▮▮▮▮▮▮▮
between the lines to delete it.

Also, since these blank spaces are characters, you can actually change the size of them (font size, that is), as well as the *leading* (space between the lines), the style, the paragraph spacing, etc. This comes in handy for manipulating space.

Centering Text

And a most important thing: when you **center** a word or line, Mac takes all those blank spaces into consideration, so any spacebar spaces or any first-line indents or any tabs you've inserted will be used to calculate the center of the line, making the line not *appear* centered.

This line appears not to be centered, although it has been selected and told to be centered.

This line is centered.
This line is also centered
but it includes a tab.

The invisible tab character
that is disrupting the alignment
must be highlighted
and removed, like so:

The tab space has been selected and will now be deleted.

This line is also centered.
Then it will be centered just fine:
This line is also centered.

After deleting the invisible space, the line is now centered just fine.

Changing Fonts (Typefaces) and Rule #2

Throughout the entire Mac environment, to make any changes you must follow Rule #2:

Select First, Then Operate.

For instance, to change to a different **font,** or typeface: first *select* the type you want to change (press-and-drag over the word/s), then *choose* the font name you want to change it into. The font list is found in your menu under various labels, depending on your program.

Notice that the insertion point picks up whatever font and style and size and alignment *is directly to the left of it.* No matter where you set it down, you will type in the font, etc, of that character, even if that character is an empty space (unless you proceed as in the following paragraph).

Now, let's say you know that the next thing you're going to type is going to be in a different font. Do you need to type it first and then select it and change the font? No.

Set your insertion point down where you want to type in the new font. *While nothing is selected,* go up to the menu and choose the font (and style and size, if you like); when there is no text selected, all the formatting *gets poured into the insertion point*—whatever you type next will be in the font you just chose. As soon as you place the insertion point elsewhere, though, it will again pick up all the formatting of the character to its left.

Please see Chapter 13 for more information on fonts.

Style is referring to whether the type is plain, bold, italic, outline, etc. To change the style of the type, you need to follow Rule #2: *select first, then operate.* Select the type to be changed (highlight it), then choose the style you want from the menu. You can choose more than one of these; for instance, you can have a face that is bold-italic-outlined-shadowed type. Yuk.

Changing Style

> To remove all of the style choices at once, simply select the text and choose Plain or Normal.

As mentioned in that last section about changing *fonts,* you can choose the style you want from the menu *before* you type it (as long as you don't move the insertion point after choosing). But even that's a pain if you just want to italicize the next word and then return to normal text. This is the preferred method:

Notice the keyboard shortcuts in the style menu? They are almost always Command–**B** for Bold, Command–**I** for Italic, etc. (Some programs may use Command–Shift–B and Command–Shift–I, etc.).

Changing Styles Mid-Stream— Without Using the Menu

> As you're typing along, simply press Command–**B** and the next word you type will be **bold**; when you want the next word to be *not* bold, press Command–**B** again and it will take *off* the bold (that's called a *toggle switch,* when choosing the same command turns that command off). Logically, you can press Command–**B**–**I** to create a word that is (guess!) ***bold italic.***

Size in type is measured in *points*. Points, in the traditional type world outside of personal computers, are each $1/72$ of an inch. The Macintosh developers were brilliant in designing the Mac screen so each pixel, or dot on the screen, is $1/72$ of an inch—type sizes are quite true to what those who deal with traditional type are accustomed to.

Changing Type Size

In your menu you see different numbers referring to the size of type; logically, the bigger the number, the bigger the type. Again, to change the size: *select first, then operate.* Or set your insertion point down and choose the size from the menu *before* you type (see the last two sections on changing fonts and styles). For more information on type sizes, see the next chapter on fonts.

Alignment

Alignment refers to where the margins are lined up: *align left* has the left margin lined up; *align right* has the right, obviously; *align center* has everything centered on a vertical axis *between your margins; justified* has both the left *and* right margins lined up. To change your alignment, you know what to do! That's right: *select first, then operate*—highlight the text, then choose the alignment.

A note when centering: If you have a first-line indent or tabs in the text that is to be centered, or if you have inserted blank spaces either before or after the text, then those spaces are taken into consideration when centering; Mac sees them as characters. So if your centered text doesn't look centered, select and remove any extra space (see page 42).

Cut, Copy, and the Clipboard

Almost anywhere you can type, you can cut or copy text. When you **cut** text, it is *removed* from your document and placed on the Clipboard. When you **copy** text, the original *is left on your document* and a *copy* of it is placed on the clipboard. Well, what the heck is the Clipboard?

The Clipboard: The Clipboard is a little "container" somewhere in the depths of the Mac. In some programs you can ask to *Show the Clipboard,* in which case it appears as a window with its contents displayed. In most programs, though, you never see it; you just must trust that it's there. (If you have the Clipboard system icon in your System Folder, then it's there in every application.)

The Clipboard holds whatever you have cut or copied, be it text, spreadsheet data, graphics, etc. Once something is on the Clipboard, it waits there until you paste it in somewhere (you'll get to that in the next paragraph). **The most important thing to remember about the Clipboard** is that it holds *only one thing at a time;* that is, as soon as you cut or copy something else, whatever was in the Clipboard to begin with is *replaced* with the new selection.

The Clipboard
holds only one item
at a time.

The Clipboard appears as a window (if it's available for looking at)

Items will stay on the Clipboard even when you change applications; you can put something on the Clipboard in a paint program, then open up a word processing program and paste it into a new document. Items will leave the Clipboard all by themselves if the computer is turned off or if there is a power failure; the contents are stored in RAM, so anytime RAM gets wiped out, so do the contents of the Clipboard. (RAM info on page 63).

Cut

How to Cut: Simply select, then operate; that is, select the text you wish to remove from the document (press-and-drag over it). Then from the Edit menu choose "Cut." It will be *eliminated* from your document and placed on the Clipboard. (Be sure to read "Delete" further on in this section.)

Copy

How to Copy: Simply select, then operate; that is, select the text you wish to copy (press-and-drag over it), then from the Edit menu choose "Copy." It will *remain* on your document and a *copy* will be placed on the Clipboard.

Paste

OK—it's on the Clipboard. Now what? Well, the Clipboard holds it for **pasting.** You can take text or graphics out of one place and paste it into your document somewhere else, just as if you had a little glue pot.

How to Paste: With text, simply set the insertion point down where you want the Clipboard item to appear; from the Edit menu choose "Paste." Whatever was on the Clipboard will be inserted in your document *beginning at the flashing insertion point.* Spreadsheet data, graphics, etc., all can be pasted in also.

As long as something is on the Clipboard, you can paste it in a million times.

Backspace/ Delete or Clear and the Clipboard

Now, **Backspace** or **Delete** is a little different: if you hit this key (upper right of keyboard) while something is selected, whatever is selected is *deleted* and is *not* placed on the Clipboard. This means it won't replace what you have on the Clipboard, if you are saving something there to paste in again, but it also means that you don't have it anymore—it is really gone. **Clear,** sometimes found in the Edit menu, does the same thing.

Undo

Undo can sometimes save your boompah (no, that's not computer jargon—it's Grandma's euphemism). When you do something that makes you scream, "Aack! Oh no!" then try Undo. It's always in the Edit menu at the top of the list (or use Command-Z).

What Undo can undo is *only the last action that occurred.* For instance, if you selected two paragraphs of brilliantly witty text that you spent three hours composing and just then the cat walked across your keyboard and obliterated the entire work, Undo could give it back to you **IF** you asked to Undo before you touched anything. If you start fiddling around with the keys and the mouse, then what you will undo is that fiddling around. So if something goes wrong, the first thing to do is **UNDO.**

Command–Z X C V

Thoughtfully, the Mac designers have made the keyboard shortcuts for the cut/copy/paste/undo commands very handy. Notice on your keyboard the letters **Z, X, C,** and **V,** all in a row right near the Command key.

• Command–**Z** will Undo (the closest to the ⌘ key).
• Command–**X** will Cut (X like eXiting or Xing it out).
• Command–**C** will Copy (C for Copy, easy mnemonic).
• Command–**V** will Paste (V because it is next to C).

It's nice to get familiar with these. Remember, select first (*except to Undo*); then hold down the Command key while pressing the other letter.

Accessing Special Characters

Special characters are the symbols you have access to on the Macintosh that aren't available on a typewriter, such as upside-down question marks for Spanish (¿), the pound symbol for English money (£), the cents sign (¢), the registration or trademark symbols (® ™), etc. You

can view all these with your **Key Caps** desk accessory.
(If you aren't sure what Key Caps is, please read page 82.)

To get special characters into your document, follow
these steps:

- While working in your document, pull down the
  desk accessory Key Caps from the Apple menu
  (far left; press on the apple).

- From the Key Caps menu (a new item that appears
  now on the right!) choose the font you wish to view.

- Find the character you want by pressing Shift **or**
  Option **or** Shift-Option together; press the character
  key; notice what combination of keystrokes produces
  the character you want. For instance, Shift-Option- ~
  (tilde key) in the font Geneva will produce a bunny
  rabbit: 🐰

- So *remember* that keystroke combination; close up
  Key Caps to get back to your document (remember,
  you can access desk accessories in any program).

- In your document, set your insertion point down;
  choose the font Geneva and the size 12 point; press
  Shift-Option- ~. The bunny will appear!

Another way to accomplish this is to press Shift-Option-~
in whatever font you are currently using; some strange
character will appear. Select the strange character and
change it into Geneva 12 point; it will turn into a bunny.

You can also select and copy the character showing in
the Key Caps entry bar—select as you would any text,
and copy from the Edit menu. Back at your document,
set the insertion point and paste it in. Unfortunately,
if your document text is another font, the Key Caps
characters will pick up that font. You will still have to
select the new characters and change them into the font
that held those characters you wanted. It seems easier
just to do it the other way.

Remember, the insertion point picks up the
*formatting of any character immediately to its left, even
if it's a blank space*, so anything else you type will
be in that character's font, style, etc. To continue
in your *original* font, leave your insertion point

Using Key Caps

*Some special characters
and the keys to
access them:*

- •   Option - 8
- ©   Option - g
- ™   Option - 2
- ®   Option - r
- ¢   Option - $
- °   Option - Shift - 8
- ... Option - ;
- –   Option - hyphen
- —   Option - Shift - hyphen

*Just For Fun—using
Shift-Option-Tilde (~)*

- ♥   New York 9 pt.
- ⌣   New York 10 pt.
- 🤖   New York 12 pt.
- ♪   New York 14 pt.
- ⌗   Geneva 9 pt.
- 📧   Geneva 10 pt.
- 🐰   Geneva 12 pt.
- ☰   Monaco 9 pt.
- �
   Monaco 14 pt.
-    Athens 14 pt.

❗

right where it is; from the menu just choose the font specifications you were originally using.

Using Accent Marks

Included in your special characters are **accent marks,** such as those in résumé and piñata. You can find them in Key Caps, but it's easy to remember that they're accessed using the Option key and are hiding beneath the characters on the keyboard that would usually be under them; e.g. the accent acute over the **e** is Option-e; the tilde over the **n** is Option-n.

A list of common accent marks:

´	Option – e
`	Option – ~
¨	Option – u
~	Option – n
^	Option – i

To type accent marks in your document, follow these steps (using the word résumé):

- Type the word until you come to the letter that will be *under* the accent mark; e.g. **r**

- *Before* you type that letter (the letter **e** in this case), type the Option combination (**Option-e** in this case)—*it will look like nothing happened.*

- Now type the character that is to be *under* the accent mark, and both the mark and the letter will appear together; e.g. **r é s u m é**

- That's easy, huh!

One Space After Periods

What?! One space after a period? If you grew up on a typewriter, this is not an easy habit to change. But characters on a Macintosh are not *monospaced* as they are on a typewriter (except for Monaco and Courier), so there is no longer the need to use two spaces to separate two sentences. Take a look at the font Courier on page 56; notice the spacing of its letters as opposed to the Times font above it. You can see why a font like that needs two spaces after periods. Check any book or magazine on your shelf; you will never find two spaces after periods (except books produced on a computer typed by someone still using typewriter rules).

A Commercial

If you are typing on a Macintosh, you must face the fact that it is not a typewriter and that some of the standard conventions developed particularly for that wonderful little appliance do not apply to the kind of type you are now creating. A very important book to read is The Mac is not a typewriter *by the same author and publisher as this book. It's small, it's cheap, it's easy to read, and it's true.*

CHAPTER THIRTEEN

FONTS

In the Mac environment, the term **fonts** refers to the typefaces available. Technically, that's not exactly what it means traditionally, but we'll let it pass rather than confuse the issue.

Certain fonts are standard with the System that comes with your Macintosh:

Geneva	Helvetica
New York	Times
Monaco	Courier
Chicago	Symbol (Greek & other characters)
Venice	

The list is separated into two columns intentionally—do you notice anything funny about them? No? Well, it's this: one list is all **city names;** the other is not. Big deal, you say.

Actually, it is a big deal. The Mac can print to basically three kinds of **printers:** the ImageWriter, with a lower resolution of about 75 dots per inch; the laserwriters, with higher resolutions of 300 to 400 dots per inch; and the high-end machines such as the Linotronic, with very high resolutions of around 2000 dots per inch. *The higher the resolution, the clearer and sharper the printed letters look.* What you are reading right now is from a Linotronic. Macintosh fonts are either *bit-mapped*—designed for low resolution, like the ImageWriter; or *PostScript,* designed for high resolution, like the LaserWriter or Linotronic. The city names clue you to which font works best with which type of printer.

The typefaces Helvetica and Times are very popular, standard typefaces in **traditional** type, which the Mac is emulating. Courier is monospaced and shaped like a typical typewriter font. These three, plus Greek Symbols, are installed in the Macintosh system, *as well as in the LaserWriter,* the printer with the higher resolution of 300 dots per inch. They look very nice when printed on the LaserWriter or any of the high-end printers.

Name Associations

Now, what city do you **associate** with The Times? New York, you say? (Actually, Times was invented for The London Times, but we're in America, so...) How right you are! *New York is the bit-mapped, ImageWriter version of Times.* Times has been redesigned into New York to look as clean as possible for the lower resolution of the Macintosh screen (72 dots per inch) and for the ImageWriter printer (approximately 75 dots per inch).

This'll stump you—what country is the typeface Helvetica named after? Wrong again, dear— *Confederatio Helvetia* is what Switzerland calls herself. Do you see a font with a city-name associated with Switzerland? Of course: Geneva. *Geneva is the bit-mapped ImageWriter version of Helvetica.*

And for some reason as yet unfathomable, the bit-mapped ImageWriter version of Courier (which looks like a typewriter and why anyone would want to use a LaserWriter to make their work look like a typewriter is a mystery) is Monaco.

Other Installed Fonts

Other *PostScript* fonts are also **installed** into the *Laser-Writer,* so if you have bought them and they are installed in your *System* you can use them without any trouble.

Palatino	Bookman
Avant Garde	New Century Schoolbook
Zapf Chancery	Zapf Dingbats: ▲ ♥ ✿ ➪

(Zapf Chancery, by the way, was designed by a German, Hermann Zapf, but modeled on an old Italian calligraphy. Its ImageWriter version is Venice, an Italian city. Zapf Dingbats: *dingbats* is a technical printers'/typographers' term referring to those little tiny pictures.)

The fonts that don't come with your System are things you have to buy; they come on a disk and must be installed into your system with a Font/DA Mover. Apple provides a Font/DA Mover on one of the disks that arrived with your Mac (see Chapter 14 to learn how to work with the Mover).

Important Information

That's a lot of very interesting trivia, you say, but so what? Well, the important thing to remember about all this is the cardinal rule:

Never use a typeface with a city name on the LaserWriter.

What happens is the LaserWriter can't read bit-mapped fonts, so it has to *create* them when you print. Many programs will automatically substitute Times for New York, Helvetica for Geneva, and Courier for Monaco, fooling you into thinking you have the real LaserWriter font. Have you ever seen (or produced) work on a LaserWriter where the words had awkward gaps between them, the numbers didn't line up, the tabs didn't line up, the shift-line was broken, or they looked almost as raggedy as on the screen? **That's the result of printing city-named fonts on the LaserWriter.**

This is an example of 9 pt. New York from the LaserWriter with no font substitution.

This is an example of 9 pt. New York from the LaserWriter with automatic font substitution.

This is an example of 9 pt. Times from the LaserWriter. It doesn't need font substitution.

The bit-mapped city-named fonts were designed (and actually look better than the others) for the *ImageWriter*. So it's best to keep each one where they belong.

The **type size** listings in the Mac also have a little vagary that's nice to know about. Have you noticed how some of the sizes listed are in outline type, and some are not (see right)? This can be different for each font.

Installed sizes

What the outlined number is indicating is that this particular size for this particular font has been *installed* in the System. It will look its best on the screen in the outlined size, and will print best on the ImageWriter in the outlined size. You can ask for any other size, and in some programs type in your own size up to 127 point or beyond, but it'll look funky. The bigger, the funkier. And if it looks funky on the screen, it will look funky on the ImageWriter, because the ImageWriter can only reproduce what it sees on the screen.

The LaserWriter, on the other hand, can create a PostScript font *(not a city name)* in any size you like. So even if it looks totally gross on the screen, the LaserWriter will print it as neatly at 95 point as it will at 12 point (as, of course, will any PostScript machine). Note the example on the next page.

57 point Times on the screen and printed on the ImageWriter **R**   R *57 point Times printed on the LaserWriter*

If you acquire more screen sizes (or entire fonts, for that matter), you can install them with your Font/DA Mover (see Chapter 14).

Screen fonts and Printer fonts

Fonts
Icon that holds screen fonts

Bit-mapped fonts, which are those fonts designed for the ImageWriter and which usually have a city name, have only one part to them—the **screen font** itself. Since the ImageWriter prints what it sees on the screen, the *screen font* contains all the necessary information. Once the *screen font* is installed in the System (it will show up in your font list), you're ready to type and print with it.

NewBasRom
Icon representing a printer font
(ITC New Baskerville Roman)

PostScript fonts, however (those designed for printers such as the LaserWriter), have two separate parts—a *screen font* and a corresponding **printer font.** When you acquire new PostScript fonts, you must install the *screen font* with the Font/DA mover, just as with bit-mapped fonts; you must **also** put the *printer font* icon into the System Folder. *Printer font icons* cannot be inside any other folder inside the System Folder or the printer won't be able to find them.

The PostScript LaserWriter fonts listed in this chapter have their printer fonts installed directly into the LaserWriter's read-only memory, so you needn't worry about their printer icons.

More Examples

On the following pages are examples of the fonts that are supplied with your System, and also the other fonts that are installed in the LaserWriter.

(Notice the apostrophes printed in these examples! See page 88 if you are interested—which you should be—in how to type apostrophes and quotation marks.)

ImageWriter fonts on the ImageWriter; Faster Quality; Tall Adjusted

Geneva (10 point)

Plain: The quick brown fox jumps over the lazy dog's back.
Bold: The quick brown fox jumps over the lazy dog's back.
Italic: The quick brown fox jumps over the lazy dog's back.
Bld Ital: The quick brown fox jumps over the lazy dog's back.

New York (10 point)

Plain: The quick brown fox jumps over the lazy dog's back.
Bold: The quick brown fox jumps over the lazy dog.
Italic: The quick brown fox jumps over the lazy dog's back.
Bld Ital: The quick brown fox jumps over the lazy dog.

Monaco (9 point)

Plain: The quick brown fox jumps over the lazy dog's back.
Bold: The quick brown fox jumps over the lazy dog.
Italic: The quick brown fox jumps over the lazy dog's back.
Bdl tal: The quick brown fox jumps over the lazy dog.

Chicago (10 point)

Plain: The quick brown fox jumps over the lazy dog's back.
Bold: The quick brown fox jumps over the lazy dog.
Italic: The quick brown fox jumps over the lazy dog's back.
Bld Ital: The quick brown fox jumps over the lazy dog.

Venice (10 point)

Plain: The quick brown fox jumps over the lazy dog's back.
Bold: The quick brown fox jumps over the lazy dog.
Italic: The quick brown fox jumps over the lazy dog's back.
Bld Ital: The quick brown fox jumps over the lazy dog.

ImageWriter fonts on the LaserWriter • no font substitution

(The lines are drawn in, as opposed to using the underline function)

Geneva (10 point)

Plain: The quick brown fox jumps over the lazy dog's back.
Bold: **The quick brown fox jumps over the lazy dog's back.**
Italic: *The quick brown fox jumps over the lazy dog's back.*
Bld Ital: ***The quick brown fox jumps over the lazy dog's back.***

New York (10 point)

Plain: The quick brown fox jumps over the lazy dog's back.
Bold: **The quick brown fox jumps over the lazy dog.**
Italic: *The quick brown fox jumps over the lazy dog's back.*
Bld Ital: ***The quick brown fox jumps over the lazy dog.***

Monaco (9 point)

Plain: The quick brown fox jumps over the lazy dog's back.
Bold: The quick brown fox jumps over the lazy dog .
Italic: The quick brown fox jumps over the lazy dog's back.
BdItal:The quick brown fox jumps over the lazy dog.

Chicago (10 point)

Plain: **The quick brown fox jumps over the lazy dog's back.**
Bold: **The quick brown fox jumps over the lazy dog.**
Italic: **The quick brown fox jumps over the lazy dog's back.**
Bld Ital: **The quick brown fox jumps over the lazy dog.**

Venice (10 point)

Plain: The quick brown fox jumps over the lazy dog's back.
Bold: **The quick brown fox jumps over the lazy dog.**
Italic: *The quick brown fox jumps over the lazy dog's back.*
Bld Ital: ***The quick brown fox jumps over the lazy dog.***

ImageWriter fonts on the LaserWriter • automatic font substitution

(The lines were created using the underline function; notice how awful they look, crowding the words.
Also notice the awkward word spacing)

Geneva (10 point)
Plain: The quick brown fox jumps over the lazy dog's back.
Bold: The quick brown fox jumps over the lazy dog's back.
Italic: The quick brown fox jumps over the lazy dog's back.
Bld Ital: The quick brown fox jumps over the lazy dog's back.

New York (10 point)
Plain: The quick brown fox jumps over the lazy dog's back.
Bold: The quick brown fox jumps over the lazy dog.
Italic: The quick brown fox jumps over the lazy dog's back.
Bld Ital: The   quick brown fox jumps over the lazy dog.

Monaco (9 point)
Plain: The quick brown fox jumps over the lazy dog's back.
Bold: The quick brown fox jumps over the lazy dog.
Italic: The quick brown fox jumps over the lazy dog's back.
BdItal: The quick brown fox jumps over the lazy dog.

Chicago (10 point)
Plain: The quick brown fox jumps over the lazy dog's back.
Bold: The quick brown fox jumps over the lazy dog.
Italic: The quick brown fox jumps over the lazy dog's back.
Bld Ital: The quick brown fox jumps over the lazy dog.

Venice (10 point)
Plain: The quick brown fox jumps over the lazy dog's back.
Bold: The quick brown fox jumps over the lazy dog.
Italic: The quick brown fox jumps over the lazy dog's back.
Bld Ital: The quick brown fox jumps over the lazy dog.

LaserWriter fonts on the LaserWriter • no font substitution

(The lines are drawn in, as opposed to using the underline function)

Helvetica (12 point)

Plain: The quick brown fox jumps over the lazy dog's back.

Bold: **The quick brown fox jumps over the lazy dog's back.**

Italic: *The quick brown fox jumps over the lazy dog's back.*

Bold Ital: ***The quick brown fox jumps over the lazy dog's back.***

Times (12 point)

Plain: The quick brown fox jumps over the lazy dog's back.

Bold: **The quick brown fox jumps over the lazy dog's back.**

Italic: *The quick brown fox jumps over the lazy dog's back.*

Bold Ital: ***The quick brown fox jumps over the lazy dog's back.***

Courier (12 point)

```
Plain:  The brown fox jumps over the lazy dog.
Bold:   The brown fox jumps over the lazy dog.
Italic: The brown fox jumps over the lazy dog.
Bld Itl: The brown fox jumps over the lazy dog.
```

Symbol (12 point)

Plain: Τηε θυιχκ βροων φοξ φυμπσ οϖερ τηε λαζψ δογΠσ βαχκ.

Bold: Τηε θυιχκ βροων φοξ φυμπσ οϖερ τηε λαζψ δογΠσ βαχκ.

Italic: Τηε θυιχκ βροων φοξ φυμπσ οϖερ τηε λαζψ δογΠσ βαχκ.

Bold Ital: Τηε θυιχκ βροων φοξ φυμπσ οϖερ τηε λαζψ δογΠσ βαχκ.

Palatino (12 point)

Plain: The quick brown fox jumps over the lazy dog's back.

Bold: **The quick brown fox jumps over the lazy dog's back.**

Italic: *The quick brown fox jumps over the lazy dog's back.*

Bold Ital: ***The quick brown fox jumps over the lazy dog's back.***

More LaserWriter fonts on the LaserWriter

Avant Garde (12 point)

Plain: The quick brown fox jumps over the lazy dog's back.
Bold: The quick brown fox jumps over the lazy dog's back.
Italic: The quick brown fox jumps over the lazy dog's back.
Bld Ital: The quick brown fox jumps over the lazy dog's back.

Bookman (12 point)

Plain: The quick brown fox jumps over the lazy dog's back.
Bold: The brown fox jumps over the lazy dog's back.
Italic: The quick brown fox jumps over the lazy dog's back.
Bld Ital: The brown fox jumps over the lazy dog's back.

New Century Schoolbook (12 point)

Plain: The quick brown fox jumps over the lazy dog's back.
Bold: The quick brown fox jumps over the lazy dog.
Italic: The quick brown fox jumps over the lazy dog's back.
Bld Ital: The quick brown fox jumps over the lazy dog.

Zapf Chancery (12 point)

Plain: The quick brown fox jumps over the lazy dog's back.
Bold: The quick brown fox jumps over the lazy dog's back.
Italic: The quick brown fox jumps over the lazy dog's back.
Bld Ital: The quick brown fox jumps over the lazy dog's back.

> No, this isn't a typographic error: Zapf Chancery is small for its size, and doesn't change styles.

Zapf Dingbats (12 point)

Plain: ✳✺✳ ❑◆✳✳✳ ❂❏❑❐■ ✳❏❙ ✳◆❍❑▲ ❑◆✳❏ ▼●
CAPS: ★★✣ ★✳☆✣☆ ✢✳✳★★ ◆★★ ❂★★☆★ ★★✣✳ ★★✣
Italic: ✳✺✳ ❑◆✳✳✳ ❂❏❑❐■ ✳❏❙ ✳◆❍❑▲ ❑◆✳❏ ▼●
Outline: ✳✺✳ ❑◇✳✳✳ ❂❏❑❐❑ ✳❏❙ ✳◇❍❑△ ❑◇✳❏ ▽●

See the Zapf Dingbats chart on page 103.

Font Sizes Below are two of the PostScript fonts shown in several sizes to give you an indication of what to expect in a particular size. They have been printed on a Linotronic. Times is a *serif;* Helvetica is a *sans serif.* (This book is set in 10 point ITC New Baskerville, with heads in 10 point Futura Bold.)

This line is set in 6 point Times.

This line is set in 8 point Times.

This line is set in 9 point Times.

This line is set in 10 point Times.

This line is set in 12 point Times.

This line is set in 14 point Times.

This line is set in 18 point Times.

This line is set in 24 point Times.

This line is 30 point Times.

This line is set in 36 pt.

This line is set in 6 point Helvetica.

This line is set in 8 point Helvetica.

This line is set in 9 point Helvetica.

This line is set in 10 point Helvetica.

This line is set in 12 point Helvetica.

This line is set in 14 point Helvetica.

This line is set in 18 point Helvetica.

This line is 24 point Helvetica.

This line is 30 pt. Helvetica.

This line is set in 36 pt.

CHAPTER FOURTEEN

FONT/DA MOVER

A **font** is a typeface. **DA** stands for **desk accessory,** the items under the Apple menu on the far left (see Chapter 20 for more info on DAs). To move fonts or desk accessories from one place to another, like from a suitcase icon to your System, or from the System on your hard disk to a System on a floppy, you need to use the Font/DA Mover. You also use this tool to *remove* them from a System.

When you buy your Mac, a Font/DA Mover is supplied on one of the disks. Typically it's stored in the System Folder or Utilities Folder, but it can be kept anywhere you like, even on a separate floppy for occasional use.

Where do you find the fonts to put in? Well, you'll notice in your System or Utilities Folder you have a little suitcase icon with a big letter A on it (you *should* have one, anyway—it may be in another folder or on one of your original disks). This icon represents the container for your screen fonts; if you double-click on it you will get the same dialog box as if you opened the Font/DA Mover.

Fonts also reside in your *System*, after they have been installed. A few are installed at the factory, and if you bought other fonts at the same time as buying your computer, the shop may install them for you.

To install or remove fonts or DAs, find the Font/DA Mover icon (as shown at the top of the right-hand column) and double-click on it. You will see the dialog box shown on the following page.

⟫

Font/DA Mover

Font/DA Mover

Where Fonts Reside

Fonts

Using the Font/DA Mover

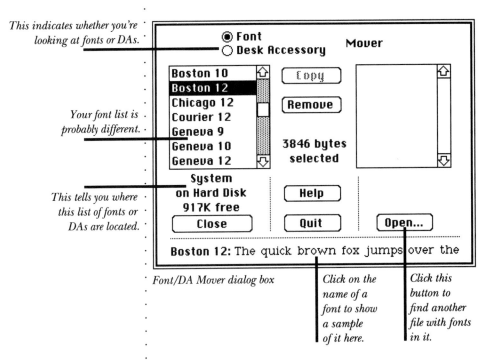

This indicates whether you're looking at fonts or DAs.

Your font list is probably different.

This tells you where this list of fonts or DAs are located.

Font/DA Mover dialog box

Click on the name of a font to show a sample of it here.

Click this button to find another file with fonts in it.

What the Font/DA Mover automatically opens up to show you are the fonts that are installed on the System that is booting (running) the machine or in the font file you just opened—you see these listed in the left-hand box. Notice the sizes listed? Those are the ones that will show up in your applications as the outlined numbers, the sizes that are installed (as noted on page 51).

On the right-hand side is an empty box above a button labeled "Open." This is waiting for you to open another font file so you can transfer them back and forth. So... click on that button to get this dialog box:

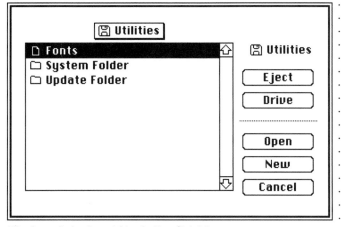

The Open dialog box within the Font/DA Mover

From this dialog box you can find the file that contains the other fonts (*Note:* The file you want may be the *System* on another disk, or the suitcase file named *Fonts,* as shown above, or perhaps it is called *Screen Fonts*):

- If the file is on a disk in another drive, click Drive to see it.

- If the file is on another disk and the current disk must be ejected to put that one in, click Eject and stick the other one in.

- When the file is visible in this box, select it by clicking once on the name; click Open; **or** simply double-click on the name to open it.

As soon as you open an appropriate file, you get back to the original dialog box (as shown on the previous page); this time the *right*-hand box will have all the fonts from the file you just chose.

At this point you simply select the fonts from either side that you want to copy or remove (select them by clicking once on them), then choose "Copy" or "Remove." You can use shift-clicking here to select more than one font at a time to copy—hold the Shift key down while clicking on or dragging over all your choices; they can all be copied or removed simultaneously.

Copying or Removing Desk Accessories

Desk Accessories

Macintosh desk accessories are also stored in a little suitcase icon or in the System. Accessories you buy from an outside source often have their own icon.

Copying or **removing** desk accessories works exactly the same as with fonts; just be sure to click the button at the top of the Font/DA Mover dialog box to select DAs instead of Fonts.

A Note About Families, Fonts, and Styles

Macintosh uses some of the typographic terminology in a slightly different way than traditionally, particularly in the way it defines "font." As an example (which is consistent with the other Macintosh fonts), one of your fonts is named Times. Times is actually a generic *family* name; in the Times *family* you have regular, italic, bold, and bold italic; technically, each one of these *members* of the family is a separate font each with its own separate group of characters. In the Macintosh environment, when you are working with the typefaces installed in the LaserWriter, the *family* name, such as Times, is considered the *font* name; the variations such as bold or italic are considered *styles*. It is important to know, though, that this is a Macintosh convention, because…

A Note About Downloadable Fonts

When you buy fonts that are *not installed in the LaserWriter* (any font without a city name other than the ones listed in the Font chapter), you often cannot change the *style* from the menu; these other typefaces follow standard convention and *each different style is considered a separate font* and must be treated as such. For example, if you are using Futura and want to italicize a word, you must choose the *font* Futura Italic from the font list—you cannot simply choose "italic" from the Format or Style menu. Now, this is not always true—font technology is changing so rapidly and the standards are not defined yet and everybody is fighting everybody else for supreme font power. If you will be using typefaces other than the standard installed ones, be sure to read about and understand them—they are usually termed *downloadable* fonts, as they must be downloaded into the LaserWriter in order to use them. There are several books available that deal just with the topic of fonts and how to install, download, and use them.

CHAPTER FIFTEEN

SAVING

Saving is the process of transferring your document from the temporary memory storage it is initally stored in to the floppy disk or hard disk where it becomes permanent. It is **extremely important** to save your document as soon as you begin working on it, and to continue to update the save *every few minutes.*

Until you actually go through the process of naming a document and saving it, the document is stored in **RAM,** which is **Random Access Memory.** This is sort of like your desk: in the filing cabinet (comparable to your disk) you have all your folders of information. But when you are working on a project, you don't keep running back to the filing cabinet every time you need a little piece of information, do you? No, you take out all the applicable info and put it on your desk, then when you're finished you put it all away again and take out something else. RAM is sort of like that: when you open an application the computer puts a copy of that application into RAM. When you close that application and open another one, Mac puts the first one back where it came from and puts the new one into RAM. That way it doesn't have to keep going into the filing cabinet to do its work and it can operate much more efficiently.

When you create a document, it sits in RAM, too, until you put it in the filing cabinet—your disk. You put it on your disk by **saving** it. Once it's on your disk, either hard or floppy, it will stay there until you trash it yourself.

While your document is in RAM, though, it is in **danger.** At any moment, if there is a power failure, even for a split second, or you accidentally hit the wrong button, or you have a system crash, or the screen freezes, or a virus attacks, or any other catastrophe of considerable dimension happens to befall, then everything in RAM (what is commonly called *memory*), is gone. Just plain gone. No way on earth for a mortal person to get it back.

The prevention? **SOS:** Save Often, Stupid. Well, that's a little harsh—how about Save Often, Smartie. Save Save Save. Every few minutes, when you're just sitting there thinking about your next marvelous move, Save. In most

Saving

RAM:
Random Access
Memory

Danger!

Rule #1:
Save Often!

programs it's as easy as pressing Command–S. Then
if there *is* a catastrophe, you will have lost only the last
few minutes of your work.

Save As...
vs. Save

To initally save a document, it must be given a name.
Under the File menu are the commands **Save As...**
and **Save.** At first the subtle difference can be confusing.

Save As...

Save As... is the command you must use *first* in order
to give the document a name, as a document cannot be
saved without a name; "Save As..." gives you a dialog box
such as the one shown below (they're slightly different
from program to program).

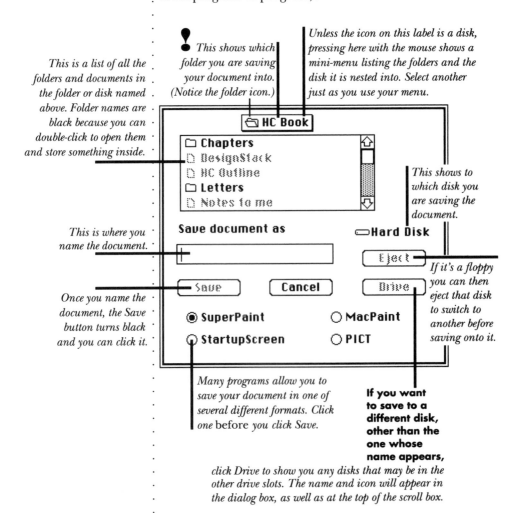

*This shows which
folder you are saving
your document into.
(Notice the folder icon.)*

*Unless the icon on this label is a disk,
pressing here with the mouse shows a
mini-menu listing the folders and the
disk it is nested into. Select another
just as you use your menu.*

*This is a list of all the
folders and documents in
the folder or disk named
above. Folder names are
black because you can
double-click to open them
and store something inside.*

*This shows to
which disk you
are saving the
document.*

*This is where you
name the document.*

*Once you name the
document, the Save
button turns black
and you can click it.*

*If it's a floppy
you can then
eject that disk
to switch to
another before
saving onto it.*

☞ HC Book

☐ Chapters
☐ DesignStack
☐ HC Outline
☐ Letters
☐ Notes to me

Save document as

☐ Hard Disk

[Eject]

[Save]   [Cancel]   [Drive]

● SuperPaint   ○ MacPaint
○ StartupScreen   ○ PICT

*Many programs allow you to
save your document in one of
several different formats. Click
one before you click Save.*

**If you want
to save to a
different disk,
other than the
one whose
name appears,**
*click Drive to show you any disks that may be in the
other drive slots. The name and icon will appear in
the dialog box, as well as at the top of the scroll box.*

Save is what you use *after* it has been named and you want to save the new changes onto that document. *Save* just goes ahead and does it—you won't see or hear anything. You must just trust.

> There is no keyboard shortcut listed in the menu for "Save as…." But if you have not yet given the document a name, then choosing *Save* (keyboard shortcut ⌘–S) will give you the *Save As…* dialog box because it must have a name. Some programs will not even allow the name "Untitled."

If you want to create changes in a document, but want to keep a copy of the original *without* the changes, then use *Save As…* a *second* time to give the document a *new* name. This puts the original document safely away on your disk and opens a new one (the copy) right where you are. You'll notice the name in the window title bar of your document will change to what you renamed it. Any changes you make to *this* document will not affect the original.

Also, if you made a bunch of changes you don't want, simply close the document and *don't save the changes.* Reopen it and everything will be exactly the way it was last time you saved.

Occasionally a program will have the option to **Revert** in the File menu; this will revert you back to the last version you saved without having to close the current file.

Save

Making Several Versions

Reverting to the Last-Saved Version

CHAPTER SIXTEEN

PRINTING

Printing is the process of copying your data from inside the Macintosh onto a piece of paper; this piece of paper, then, in computer jargon, is called "hard copy."

Printing

The **ImageWriter** printer is the one people typically have at home because it isn't very expensive (relatively speaking, anyway). It's a dot-matrix printer (75 dots per inch), but it looks much better than most of the dot-matrix printers we've all seen over the years. On page 53 is an example of the ImageWriter quality using the fonts installed in the Mac.

Printers

The **LaserWriter** is the printer that made desktop publishing happen. It takes the same document that was printed on the ImageWriter and outputs it with a much higher resolution (300 dots per inch) and much blacker black. Examples of LaserWriter copy are on pages 54–57.

There are also very expensive (like $80,000), very high-end printers with resolutions of around 2000 dots per inch, such as the **Linotronic.** These printers output onto film, not paper, and the hard copy looks virtually like traditional typesetting, limited only by the professional expertise of the person who input the type. This book was output on a Linotronic.

Since the high resolution machines are so expensive, you only find them in a *service bureau*—a shop where they offer the output as a service. You would take the disk containing your document to them, leave it there, and they would print it up for you. It can cost from $6 to $10 a page, but it's beautiful.

Please read Chapter 13 on Fonts before you print your document. Printing to your ImageWriter or LaserWriter is very simple. Your application may give you different print dialog boxes depending on which printer you are connected to, and the dialog boxes within different applications may look slightly different, but basically all you need to do is answer the questions they ask.

Preparing to Print

The first thing you want to do is to **Save** it again—as a preventive measure always save just before you print (one never knows when the document-eating gremlins are lurking about). Also:

- make sure the printer is turned on;
- the ImageWriter must have its "Select" button on also.

Chooser The very first time you print on your machine, or if you

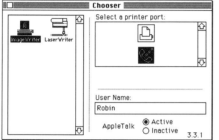

are hooked up to more than one printer, or if you go somewhere else and print, or if you find you are having difficulty printing, you may need to go to Chooser to direct the computer to the printer.

Chooser is a desk accessory that should be found under the Apple at the top left of your menu (also see page 79 for more info on this). For every printer icon in your System Folder, there will be a matching icon in your Chooser; even if you have a printer hooked-up right next to you, you won't be able to print to it unless its icon is in your System Folder.

ImageWriter icon

On the left side of the Chooser window you will see those printer icons; click on the one representing the machine you want to print to. On the right side should be a port icon or the name of a printer; click on the one you want to use. Make sure the network button (here it is Apple-Talk) on the bottom is on if you are on a network (which you would be if more than one computer is going to the same printer) and off if you are not. The LaserWriter also requires that AppleTalk be Active. Then just close the window and proceed.

LaserWriter icon

Print Dialog Boxes After your document is saved (and the printer is designated through Chooser, if necessary), just go up to the File menu and choose "Print...." Depending on your application, you'll get some sort of dialog box asking you questions. Most of them are self-explanatory; the following items are some typical sorts of terms that may not be so obvious:

Quality: Draft quality on the ImageWriter prints very quickly, but eliminates any graphics you may have had and produces really awful stuff; you can generally ignore this option unless you're in an extreme hurry and don't care at all what it looks like.

You can adjust the draft quality with the button on the ImageWriter itself. If you turn off the Select light, you can push the Print Quality button to one of the three levels shown. You'll get three levels of terrible type, from awful to worse.

Orientation: Your application may use another term for it, but what Mac wants to know is if it should print upside right or sideways (8.5 x 11 or 11 x 8.5); also known as Tall or Wide, Portrait or Landscape.

Pages: All or **From __ to __:** You can choose to print *all* the pages contained in your document, or just pages 3 through 12 (or whatever your choice is, of course). Choosing **All** will override any numbers in the **From/To** boxes.

50% Reduction: This will print your work at half size. Remember, half of an 8.5 x 11 is 4.25 x 5.5—you must halve *both* directions. On paper, this looks like the image is ¼ the original size; it isn't—it's half of *both* the horizontal *and* the vertical.

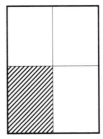

The shaded portion is 50% of the larger size— half of both the width **and** *the length.*

Tall Adjusted: The Macintosh screen has a resolution of 72 dots per inch; the ImageWriter prints at 75 dots per inch. Thus the ImageWriter tends to print large circles, such as pie charts, in oval shapes; choosing Tall Adjusted will fix that. It will also more closely resemble LaserWriter spacing; if you're using the ImageWriter as draft copies for eventual production on the LaserWriter, this will help judge the work a little better. And it looks nicer anyway.

Computer Paper: This does not refer to pin-fed paper! Computer paper is 11 x 13 inches. Pin-fed paper is 8.5 x 11 (letter-size, just all strung together).

When you click the last OK button, the messages will be sent to the printer and your brilliant document shall come rolling along in a short moment.

Every time you turn on a LaserWriter, it spews forth a sample page for you to check the toner level and quality, as well as letting you know how many pages have been printed on this toner cartridge. If you don't want to waste paper or toner on this page everyday, simply loosen the paper tray before you turn it on. A minute or two after the LaserWriter stops whirring, push it back in.

Save LaserWriter Toner & Paper

**Align
ImageWriter
Pin-Fed Paper**

When printing from most applications you can determine how far down from the top of the page you want the document to begin. Unfortunately, the ImageWriter doesn't know where the perforation of the pin-fed paper is; it just assumes it's at the top of the page and adjusts itself according to your specifications. In order to keep it consistent, so your documents always begin where you expect and line breaks will occur at perforations rather than in the middle of documents, do this:

1. Turn the printer on.
2. Make sure the Select light is **off.**
3. Press the line feed button until the perforation is just at the top of the printer head (if you hold the button down, after four lines it will form-feed until you let go).
4. Print your work (take notice if you need to arrange that first adjustment higher or lower; that is, above or below the printer head).
5. **When your work is finished printing, don't ever roll the paper forward manually in order to get to the perf to tear it off! That's exactly what causes the problem, because then it isn't lined up any more.**
6. Instead, turn the Select button off.
7. Press the **form-feed button;** this will roll one entire sheet out of the printer, leaving the perforation lined up exactly how you just set it in step #3.
8. Turn the Select light back on now so you don't forget, since you cannot print with the Select light off.
9. Now you can tear off your page, leaving one full sheet hanging out of the printer.

Obviously, this is going to waste one page of paper per document. But it actually wastes *less* than if your document printed right over the perforation marks and you had to reprint the whole thing! Another good aspect of doing it this way is that with that whole sheet hanging out of the printer it doesn't get curled around the roller and roll back inside itself when you try to print. You can always save the extra sheets for your kids, for scratch paper, or have the local copy shop make pads for you.

CHAPTER SEVENTEEN

CLOSING/ QUITTING

When you are finished working on a document, you can choose to **close** that particular document in order to create a brand new one to work on, or to open one that has already been created. Either way, you are just *closing the document* and remaining *within the application (the software program)*. You still see the menu belonging to the application, even though the rest of your screen may look grey, just like your Desktop.

> If you don't see "Special" in your menu, or if the trash can is not there, you have not quit—you have just *closed*, but not *quit*.

Closing A Document

🍎 File Edit View Special

If you don't see this menu, you are not at your Desktop.

To really get back to your Desktop, where the menu items are File Edit View Special, you need to **quit** the application. This is always done from the File menu, the very last item. In most programs you can use the keyboard command: ⌘ **Q.**

Quitting an Application

If you haven't saved all your changes, Mac will politely ask if you want to save them at this point, whether you are closing or quitting. Thank goodness.

If you never even initially saved the document with a name, you'll get the Save As… dialog box (page 64) to name it before quitting, because nothing can be saved without a name. If you decide at that point you don't want the document, just click the Cancel button.

> If you hold down the Option key while choosing "Quit," *and keep holding it down*, when you arrive at your Desktop all the windows will be closed!

If you are all done for the day, then close all your windows (hold the Option key down while clicking in the first close box, or try ⌘–Option–W); from the Special menu choose "Shut Down." Any disks in the drives will pop out, and you can turn off the machine with the same button you used to turn it on. (More info on Shut Down on page 73.)

Shutting Down

CHAPTER EIGHTEEN

EJECTING DISKS

There are actually many ways to eject a disk, some more preferable than others. Let's start at the Desktop.

Ejecting

If you are done for the day and are planning to shut down the whole system, then close up all your windows (Command–Option–W for System version 6.0 or higher; make sure Caps Lock is not down). From the Special menu choose "Shut Down." This will eject any floppy disks and reassuringly notify you that it is now safe to turn off the computer.

Shutting Down

Even if you're not ready to shut down, you may sometimes need to eject a floppy disk in order to trade it with another, or simply to take your disk and go away. Beginners usually go through the routine of selecting the disk (by clicking once on it) and choosing "Eject" from the File menu (or using the keyboard shortcut ⌘ **E**). This will certainly work, but it actually is not the best method.

From the Menu or the Keyboard Shortcut

You may have noticed when you eject a disk by using the menu that a grey version of the icon stays on the screen. That's because the memory of this disk is still in RAM (see page 63). If someone else comes along to use this machine while the icon is still showing, when they insert their disk the Mac will very often spit it out and ask for the one that just left. That's not a problem if the disk is sitting right there, but if Mary took that disk and left for a meeting in Chicago, then the only thing you can do, absolutely your only option, is to turn the computer off. While that dialog box is showing "Please insert the disk "Mary"," you are stuck. Mac will accept no substitutes. If you see a grey disk icon on your screen, you can try sticking it in the trash, but oftentimes even then you'll get that dialog box. Occasionally pressing Command–Period will satisfy Mac, but not often.

Grey disk icon left on the screen after being ejected

To avoid this problem, while at your Desktop it is actually preferable to *eject your disk through the trash.*

Through the Trash

Aack, you say! Yes, that's a frightening thought, but calm down; it's quite all right. *The trash can doesn't erase anything off your disk.* If you simply press on the disk icon, drag it down to the trash and put it in, your disk will safely pop out and leave no grey icon behind. The computer now has no recollection of the existence of that disk and you can merrily be on your way and no one will be mad at you for leaving yourself behind. This is especially important if more than one person uses the computer, as in an office or in a classroom.

Through Dialog Boxes

Some **dialog boxes** give you an option to eject a disk while in an application: Save As...; Open in the Font/ DA Mover; and Open in any application, to name a few. When you want to eject a disk while working, just choose something like "Save As..." even though you don't really want to rename it; choose the disk you want to eject and click the Eject button (if you don't see the name of the disk, click Drive to find it in the other drive slot). Then click the Cancel button to get back to your document.

After ejecting a disk in this way, you can of course insert a new disk if you like. If something from the ejected disk is still open on the screen, though, Mac will ask for the ejected disk again so she can put it away.

More Keyboard Shortcuts

• To eject a disk from the internal drive at any time, in any application, press Command–Shift–1 (that's the numeral One).

• To eject a disk from the external drive at any time, press Command–Shift–2.

• For a Mac with two internal drives and an external: Command–Shift–1 ejects the bottom internal drive; Command–Shift–2 ejects the top internal drive; Command–Shift–0 ejects the external drive.

The Mouse Trick

If for some reason, perhaps because of a power outage or a system error, when you turn off the computer your disk is still inside, do this:

Hold down the mouse button; *while holding it down,* turn the computer back on; your disk/s should pop out like toast.

The PaperClip Trick

If all else fails, notice that tiny hole next to the drive slot? That's paperclip size. Unbend a paperclip and push it in. It's pretty safe, as all you're doing is releasing the mechanism that holds the disk in place—you do have to push quite firmly, though.

CHAPTER NINETEEN

SHUTTING DOWN

Shutting down is the process of the computer tying up all the loose ends inside itself and parking the hard disk before it's turned off. You *can* turn it off without shutting down, but it's not recommended.

When you're done with the Macintosh, it's **good house-keeping** to close up all your windows on the desktop. If you have System 6.0 or above you can press Command–Option–W and all the windows will fly away home (make sure the Caps Lock key is not down). If you have an earlier System version, then hold down the Option key while you close the active window; all the rest will follow.

Once all the windows are closed, from the Special menu choose "Shut Down." All your disks will pop out and you'll get a reassuring dialog box telling you that you can now turn off your computer safely.

Turn it off with the same button you turned it on, and away you go! On any of the Mac IIs, "Shut Down" will also automatically turn off the computer.

Shutting Down

Good Housekeeping

CHAPTER TWENTY

DESK ACCESSORIES

Desk accessories (DAs) are handy little tools found in your menu under the Apple, designed to make life easier. Access them like any other menu item—slide down the list until it's highlighted, then let go. They're all windows, so they can be moved around the screen from their title bars and closed with their little close boxes. They all work from within the System, so you can open any of them while you are in any application.

You can buy an amazing number of desk accessories, many for very low prices. They do all manner of useful and useless things. This list explains just the ones that come standard with any Mac.

The **Alarm Clock** won't wake you up in the morning, but it will beep at you while you're sitting at your computer. After it beeps once, the apple in the corner flashes on and off; on the newer systems it flashes from an apple to an alarm clock. The problem with this alarm is that it doesn't turn itself off—even if you turn off the computer and come back next week, the alarm clock is still flashing; you have to go get it and turn it off yourself.

When the clock is the *active window* on your screen, you can press Command–C and **create a copy of the date and time;** set your insertion point down anywhere, even under an icon at your desktop, and press Command–V; the date and time will paste into your document, like so: 1:38:07 AM   7/5/90.

❑ **To change the settings,** begin by clicking on the tiny flag on the right; it will open up to a little control panel. After changing a setting, click anywhere in the clock window to put it into effect.

❑ **To change the time:**
  • Click on the time clock icon on the bottom left;
  • Click on the number in the middle panel that you wish to change (this will cause little up and down arrows to appear on the right);
  • Clicking on the arrows will move the time forward or backward **or**
  • You can *type* in the numbers once you select them, either from the keyboard or the keypad;

Desk Accessories

Alarm Clock

☐ 2:02:10 PM 🚩

flag

time clock

calendar

alarm clock

- Change AM or PM notation the same way.
- *Note:* you can press the Tab key to move the selection from hours to minutes to seconds, etc.

❏ **To change the date:**

- Do the same as for the time, after clicking on the little calendar icon.

Arrows with which to change the numbers

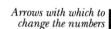
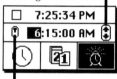

The switch to turn the alarm on or off

❏ **To set the alarm:**

- Click on the alarm clock icon;
- Change the time to when you want it to go off, as detailed above (check the AM or PM notation);
- Click the little switch on the *left* to the up position (you'll notice the zingers around the icon now);
- When the alarm goes off, you'll get a beep and/or your menu will flash, and the little apple in the menu will flash on and off.

❏ **To close up the clock:**

- To just get rid of the control panel, click on the flag in the upper right again;
- To put it away altogether, click in its close box.

❏ **To turn off the alarm:**

- To turn it off *temporarily,* but leave the alarm set for the next day at the same time, simply get the alarm clock and then click in its close box.
- To turn it off *permanently,* you must go in and reverse the process of turning it on; that is, click on the alarm clock icon and turn off the switch.

Calculator

The **Calculator** is a very handy item to have. It operates just like your hand-held calculator, although it has only the four basic functions. Remember, it's a window so it can be dragged around like any other window and put away with its close box. Access it in any application.

- Operate it with the mouse, keyboard, or keypad.
- If using the keyboard, make sure you use the real numeral 1 (one) and not a lowercase l (el).
- The division sign is the slash: **/**; the multiplication sign is the asterisk: *****
- The answer can be copied and pasted into your document using using standard methods; you don't need to select the calculator info first—if it's the active window, the Copy command knows what to copy. You can also copy numbers from your document and paste them into the Calculator.

The **Chooser** is where you choose which printer you want to print to. If you are working from a hard disk either at home or at work and are hooked up to only one printer, or if you always use the same System disk in the same computer, you need to do this only the very first time you print to that printer.

Chooser

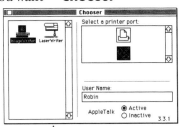

❑ Choose the icon for your printer:
  • In the left-hand box are the icons for the printers whose icons are in your System Folder;
  • Click on the icon of the printer you are going to print to (in this example it's the ImageWriter).

❑ Click on the name or the port icon of your printer:
  • Depending on which printer icon you choose on the left, in the right-hand box you'll see either names of the printers available, or port icons (the port icons are asking to which *port,* or *plug* on the back of the Mac, your printer is hooked); in the example you see the choice of a printer port or a modem port (here the modem port is chosen, as the *Laser*Writer is plugged into the printer port).

❑ Adjust the network option (a network lets more than one computer talk to the same printer; in this example it's AppleTalk):
  • If yours is the only Mac hooked up to an Image-Writer, then AppleTalk will most likely be *inactive;* if several computers are sharing the same printer **or** if you are connected to a LaserWriter, then AppleTalk should be *active.*

❑ If you type your name, you will then have the pleasure of seeing your name on the screen.

❑ Click the close box and continue to print.

Control Panel

The **Control Panel** allows you to customize the Mac to your own specific preferences, such as what kind of sound to make and how loud it is, how fast the insertion point flashes, the pattern of your Desktop, etc. What your particular Control Panel has in it depends on what system you are using and what is inside your System Folder.

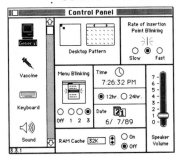

Many of the items are self-explanatory—just click

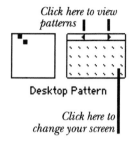

Click here to view patterns

Desktop Pattern

Click here to change your screen

on the radio buttons or on the numbers or on the words in a scroll box to alter things to your fancy. Here are a few specifics for areas that may not be so obvious:

❑ **Desktop Pattern**

- On the "Desktop Pattern" click on the tiny right and left arrows—this will take you through a variety of patterns; when you like one, click on the pattern *under* the arrows and your desktop will change; when you find the blank pattern, draw in it with the mouse to create your own—clicking on a white pixel turns it black; clicking on a black pixel turns it white, "erasing" it. All patterns can be edited.

❑ **Clock & Calendar**

- Setting the time and date here will change the Alarm Clock desk accessory also, and vice-versa.

Key Repeat Rate	Delay Until Repeat
○○○◉○	○ ○◉○○
Slow Fast	Off Long Short

❑ **Keyboard**

- Every key on the Macintosh keyboard will repeat, meaning if you hold the key down it will continue typing that character across the page. With the **Key Repeat Rate** panel you can control how fast it types that character across the screen.

- With the **Delay Until Repea**t you can turn *off* that function, so the keys will *not* repeat when you press.

- **Long** to **Short** is giving you control over *how long* you can hold your finger on a key before it starts to repeat. This is wonderful for people who are heavy on the keys—set it for a long delay so if your fingers dawdle on the keys you won't end up with extra characters all over the place.

❑ **Sound**

- Just click on one of the sounds in the list box on the right and you'll hear it at the level that you set your volume control. Whichever sound you choose last will be the one you hear whenever Mac wants to beep at you. If you don't want to hear *any* sound, set the speaker volume to zero—your menu will flash instead.

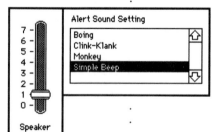

❑ **Mouse**

Click on this icon to get to its controls

- The slower you set your mouse tracking speed, with Tablet being the slowest, the farther you have to move the mouse in connection with its response on the screen. In other words, if you have a very small space for your mouse to move around in, then set this to the fastest speed—the pointer will move farther on the screen with the minimal amount of movement on the mouse pad.

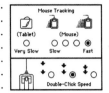

This is a most wonderful tool. There is a little man in **Find File** who will find you anything you want, even if you have no idea where it is or exactly the name of it. It may be in a folder which is in a folder which is in a folder which is in a folder. Well, this guy will go get it—he'll look in every folder on your hard drive *or* only in the folder or disk of your choice. He *won't* look in your refrigerator or under the sink.

Find File

The particular file selected here is in a folder called Works Samples, which is in a folder called Works, which is in a folder called Programs, which is on the Hard Disk.

He'll not only find your file, but if you ask him nicely he will put it on the Desktop for you. Then when you're all through and don't remember where it came from, just call him up and he will come right over and put it away for you, right back where it came from. What a guy.

❑ **To locate a file:**
- the insertion point is flashing; you need to type in at least three letters of the file name you want (actually, he will look even if you only give him one letter, but if there are too many files with that letter in it he gets mad and tells you to be more specific);
- if necessary, click on the name of the disk in the upper left to have him search another drive;
- click on the little man **or** press Return;
- you can tell him to stop looking at any time by clicking on the Stop sign with the hand on it;
- the names of any files *with those consecutive letters in it* will show up just below;
- click on the name of the file you want and in the bottom right he will tell you exactly where it is located. Make a note of where it is. If the scroll bar turns grey, press the arrow to see more.

❑ **Put the file on the Desktop:**
- you can now either close Find File and go get your

file, **or** go up to the menu bar—notice you have a new item: Find File;

• if you choose "Move to Desktop…" from that new menu, the little man gets the file for you and puts it on the Desktop.

❑ **Put the file away:**

• later, at your Desktop, when you want to put that particular file away and you don't remember where it came from, select it (by clicking once on it) and choose "Put Away" from the File menu; the little man will come and get it and put it away for you.

❑ **From inside an application:**

• if you're working on a job inside a program, then pull down Find File and enter a name in the box;

• after he makes the list for you, click on the name of the file you want;

• close the Find File window;

• now when you go to the File menu in your application to Open a document, the one the little man found for you will be waiting!

Key Caps

Key Layout

This is the icon that must be in your System Folder in order to view the special characters.

If the icon Key Layout is in your System Folder, then **Key Caps** can show you the keyboard layout for every font in your System. On a Macintosh keyboard you actually have four separate sets of keys, two of which you know already and two of which only a few people know about. You are about to become In The Know.

• after you open up Key Caps, you have a new menu item on the far right: Key Caps;

• pull down the Key Caps menu—this is a list of the fonts that are installed on your System;

• select the font you want; the characters of that font will appear on the keyboard (these are the characters everybody knows about);

• to see the Shift characters, press the Shift key (everybody knows these, too);

• to see the Option characters, press the Option key (Ha! You are now In The Know);

• to see the Shift–Option characters, press the Shift and Option keys simultaneously.

Different fonts have different characters in the other two keyboards—some have more, some have less. Most of the

Option key characters are consistent in every font, so you can always find, for instance, the accent marks or copyright, trademark, and monetary symbols, etc., in the same place.

Key Caps is only for finding the *placement* of all the available characters on the keyboard. Hold down the Option key, for instance, and see where the ¢ sign is located. Once you discover that it is found under the 4 (the $ sign, logically), then you can go back to your document and press Option and 4; the ¢ will appear. It's exactly the same idea as pressing Shift–8 to get an asterisk!

Use Key Caps for finding characters

It's possible to type the characters on the Key Caps keyboard, copy them (select the characters first, then choose Copy from the Edit menu), and then Paste them into your document (they will paste in wherever the insertion point is flashing). This works fine as long as the font you are using in your document is the same font you chose from Key Caps, or at least that they share the same character. Otherwise when you paste it in it will take on the *format* (type font, size, style) of the character to the left of the insertion point, which may not be what you want at all.

Copy & Paste

- At the Key Caps keyboard, find the character you want to use;
- remember what font and what keys to press to get that character;
- go back to your document, select the font you want, and press the appropriate keys;
- can you find the apple?

Also see pages 46–47 for more info.

The **Note Pad** is a nice little feature that allows you to write up to eight pages of notes. This is a great place to leave prearranged messages, notes about particular formatting used in a document, reminders, or more love notes. They are automatically saved (they will *not* be destroyed on rebuilding the Desktop, as Get Info notes will, p. 29)

The insertion point is flashing; type into it just as you type anywhere else in the Macintosh. You can backspace/ delete, cut, copy, paste, etc. Turn the pages by clicking on the little turned corner on the bottom left; clicking on the *very* bottom corner will turn the pages backwards.

Note Pad

```
╔══════ Note Pad ══════╗
Essays to be written:
● The three rules of life:
  1. Your attitude is your life.
  2. Maximize your options.
  3. Never take anything too
     seriously.
● Creating memories for our
  children.
● Every home should have a
  stage and dance floor.

              1
```

Click here to turn the page

Scrapbook

The **Scrapbook** is a place to permanently hold text or graphics from virtually any program; then in any other program you can take a copy of it back out from the Scrapbook and paste it into your document. Once you put something in the Scrapbook it is saved to your disk automatically. The Scrapbook holds the entire object you selected, even though you can't always see all of it in the window.

You must go through the Clipboard to put items in the Scrapbook and to take them out.

❑ **To paste something into the Scrapbook:**
- From your document, *select* and *copy* the item/s you want to place (this puts a copy on the Clipboard);
- Open the Scrapbook;
- Paste the item into the Scrapbook (from the Edit menu choose "Paste")—it will be pasted onto the page that is visible, and everything else *will move over one; nothing is being replaced*;
- Close the Scrapbook to get back to your document.

❑ **To copy an item out of the Scrapbook:**
- Open the Scrapbook
- Scroll through until the item you want *is visible;*
- Copy it (from the Edit menu choose "Copy");
- Close the Scrapbook;
- Go to your document and paste it in (usually any text that is pasted in, and sometimes graphics, will insert itself wherever the insertion point is flashing; in some programs it will just be pasted into the middle of the page).

❑ **To delete an item from the Scrapbook:**
- Scroll through until the item you want is *visible;*
- From the Edit menu choose "Clear" (Clear removes it from the Scrapbook without putting it on the Clipboard).

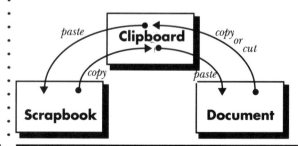

CHAPTER TWENTY-ONE

TIPS & SHORTCUTS

This is a collection of the tips or important notes that are imbedded in the rest of the book, as well as any other hints or fascinating bits of information or shortcuts that haven't been mentioned. Again, nothing is software-specific; it all relates to the general Mac environment. There's an extra page for you to add your own pieces of information as you move along with your Mac!

Caps Lock does not act like a typewriter shift-lock in that you can still type numbers while Caps Lock is down. p.18

To **move a window without making it active,** press the Command key while pressing-and-dragging in its title bar. p.20

To **align all icons horizontally** with no empty spots, hold down the Option key while choosing "Clean Up" from the Special menu. p.23

To **close all the windows** on your Desktop, hold down the Option key while clicking in the close box of the active window. p.23

On Systems 6.0 and above, you can also **close all the windows** by pressing Command–Option–W. p.23

Holding down the Option key while choosing "Quit" from any program will **close all windows on the Desktop before you even get there.** p.23

Holding down the Option key while opening folders will make those **folders close automatically when you return to the Desktop.** p.23

To **print the contents of the active window** on the ImageWriter, press Command–Shift–4. p.24

To **print the entire screen** on the ImageWriter, press Caps Lock down and Command–Shift–4. p.24

To bring the **window belonging to a grey icon** to the front, simply double-click on it. p.27

To **avoid the dialog/alert box** asking if you really want to throw away that application, hold down the Option key while trashing the icon. p.28

Compendium of Tips

The page number indicates where more information on that tip can be found.

After trashing an icon, "Empty Trash" from the Special menu in order **to free that space on the disk.** p.28

To **create a MacPaint file (a screen dump)** of anything on your screen, press Command–Shift–3. p.28

To **write notes on a file,** use the Get Info box. p.29

Hold down the **Option key to throw away a locked file.** p.30

Use folders to organize your Desktop and all your disks as you would your filing cabinet. Chapter 9 (p.31)

Create a new folder at your Desktop *before you begin* a project and **save all your related parts into that folder,** preventing them from getting misplaced. p.33, 64

To **select more than one icon** at a time, press-(in any *blank* area)-and-drag the pointer; a *marquee* will appear. Anything enclosed in this marquee will be selected. To **move them all at once,** press in any *black* area (except on the name) and drag; all the outlines will move simultaneously. p.35

Another way to **select more than one icon,** especially when the icons are not near each other, is to **Shift-Click:** press the Shift key while clicking on icons and every one you click will be selected. Conversely, **deselect** any by pressing the Shift key—only the ones you click will be deselected from the group. p.36

If you press the Option key while moving an icon from one folder to another, it will **move a copy** of it. p.36

Never hit the Return key while typing unless you really do always want the line to end at that word. p.40

If you are going to **center a line,** don't use tabs or indents or spaces before or after the line or they will make it appear off-center. p.42

While typing, **the insertion point picks up the formatting** of the character to its left—font, style, size, alignment, and ruler settings. p.43, 47

To **remove all the styles** attached to characters (bold, italic, shadowed, etc.), simply select the text and choose Plain or Normal. p.43

While typing, **use the keyboard commands to change the style** (to italic, bold, etc.) of the next word/s to be typed; choose the style again to take it off. This avoids having to select the word/s, pick up the mouse, use the menu, and set the insertion point again to continue. p.43

Don't forget about **Undo!** If something happens that you didn't want to happen or don't like, *before you do anything else,* even before you scream, **UNDO** (from the Edit menu, or Command-Z). p.46

Use the Option characters to place **accent marks** over letters. p.48

Use **only one space after sentence ends!** p.48

Never use a **typeface with a city name** on the LaserWriter. p.50–51

When saving, be sure to **save directly into the folder** you created to store your work. p.33, 64

Make **several versions of your work** using "Save As...." p.65

If you **change your mind about the changes** you just made, close the document and don't save those changes; when you reopen it, it will have reverted back to the last-saved version. p.65

To **avoid wasting paper and toner** every time you turn on your LaserWriter, pull the paper tray out a bit before you turn it on. p.69

When **ejecting disks at your desktop,** rather than ejecting them with the menu command it is preferable to drag them out through the trash can. This doesn't destroy any data on the disk, and removes the memory of that disk so the computer doesn't ask for it again. p.73

If a **disk is stuck in the computer** after the computer has been turned off, hold the mouse button down while turning the machine back on; the disk will pop out. p.74

As a **last resort to eject a disk** stuck in the computer, unroll a paperclip and push it in the tiny hole to the right of the drive slot. This will release the mechanism and pop the disk out. p.74

To **find a file**/document/application that somehow got misplaced but you know it's in there somewhere, use Find File from the Apple menu. p.81

Real Quotation Marks!

" and "

' and '

not " and '

Using inch and foot marks in place of the real quotation marks is a big problem with so much of the work that is being produced on the Mac. Yes, on the typewriters we grew up with we used those marks, but we are no longer on typewriters and are not so limited. Also, we are attempting to come close to professional type, and you never see inch and foot marks used as quotation marks in professional type. Unfortunately, they are not located in an obvious spot, so you won't know they're there unless somebody tells you. So here you are:

To create these beautiful marks in any font (and you'll always be able to find them in Key Caps), use the following keystrokes:

"	option – [
"	option – shift – [
'	option –]
'	option – shift –]

They won't always be these big round marks; each font has its own quotes designed for it. See the font lists on pages 53–57.

Return Key Shortcut

Anytime you see a double border around a button (such as the one shown below), that means you can press the Return or Enter keys to do that function, instead of picking up the mouse and clicking on it.

Replacing Highlighted Text

When text is highlighted, you don't need to delete it first in order to type in what you want. When text is highlighted, simply type; your typing will replace the highlighted word/s. This is true anywhere in the Mac—all dialog boxes, all programs, even on the Desktop when changing the name of an icon.

Ellipses... in the Menu

Three dots (the ellipsis: ...) after an item in the menu means you'll get a dialog box if you choose that item. Anything that doesn't have the ellipsis will just activate as soon as you choose it.

In any dialog box that contains boxes for you to fill in, you can press the Tab key to move you from box to box. If there is data already in the box, it will be highlighted and anything you type will replace it (you don't have to delete it first); if there is no data in the box, the Tab key will set the insertion point there, ready for you to type.

Tab in Dialog Boxes

On the front of the Macintosh, if you slip your hand right under the rainbow apple, you'll find a little roller switch that will dim or brighten your screen. It's a good idea to dim the screen if you're going to be away from the computer for a length of time, as it's possible to burn an image into the screen, just as on video games.

Dimmer Switch

There are several varieties of "screen savers" available to help avoid screen burn. A screen saver usually turns the screen black and has images that constantly move, like shooting stars or geometric shapes or fireworks. As soon as you click the mouse it disappears. Some come as desk accessories that you access through your Apple menu; some you put in your System Folder and they automatically come on after a certain period of time if the keys or mouse haven't been touched. Simply clicking the mouse will restore the screen.

Screen Savers

Several of the paint programs allow you to create a StartupScreen. Once you have a StartupScreen installed in your System Folder, every time you boot (start the computer) with that System, this image will show on the screen for a minute or two. This can be quite fun! To do it, simply create a paint document, or use clip art, and save it with the name "StartupScreen." It doesn't matter what letters are capitalized, but it does have to be one word. Put that file *into the System Folder*. The next time you boot, you'll see it!

StartupScreen

If you need to copy something from one floppy onto another floppy but your machine has only one floppy drive, this is how to do it:

Copying From One Floppy to Another Floppy with One Floppy Drive

- Insert the disk you want to copy *onto*. While it is selected (click once on it if it isn't), from the File menu choose "Eject." Remember, this ejects the disk but leaves it in RAM (p. 63). You should see the grey icon after the disk ejects.
- Insert the disk with the information to be copied from. Open it and select the files to copy: press-

and-drag them over to the grey disk (or just drag the icon of the entire disk to the other disk, which will replace *everything*).

- As Mac reads info from one disk and copies it onto the other, she will spit out disks and tell you which ones to insert next. Just follow the directions; this is called *disk-swapping*. It will eventually end.

- If you end up with a grey disk icon on the screen, just drag it out through the trash.

Rebuilding Your Desktop If you have a hard disk, you may start to notice that it slows down after a few months. This is because there is an invisible file that keeps track of all the icons that have ever been seen on your desktop, even if you just loaded them on to see what they looked like! There is a way to **rebuild** your desktop and remove all the unnecessarily-stored information. Follow these steps:

NOTE:
This process will also destroy the WDEF virus!

1. Turn off the Mac.
2. Hold down the **Command** and **Option** keys.
3. Turn the Mac back on, still holding down those keys until you see the following dialog box:

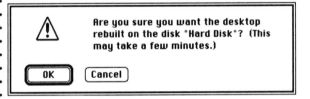

4. Click OK (or, if you read the tip on the previous page, simply hit the Return key).

- **Rebuild floppy disk desktop files** the same way: hold the Command and Option keys down while inserting a disk, until you see the above dialog box.

Mac will rebuild the desktop file for you and it should now open and close files and folders much faster, plus rid it of the rude and evil WDEF virus.

The only problem with rebuilding is that it also destroys any messages you put in your Get Info boxes. Darn it. (See page 29 for info on Get Info.)

Check Your Fonts at the Desktop To see what fonts are in the System while you are still at your Desktop, from the Apple menu choose "Key Caps." At the far right of the menu is a new menu item: Key Caps. Press on it to see the list of System fonts.

CHAPTER TWENTY-TWO

AAACK!! HELP!

This list doesn't pretend to be an all-inclusive reference for every sort of catastrophe that may befall; rather, it is just a compilation of the most common, simple problems one may encounter when first beginning to work on a Macintosh.

If the computer doesn't turn on, check *all* your switches (when the switch is labeled **1** or **0,** the **1** means **On**):

The Computer Doesn't Turn On

- If you have a floor surge-protector bar with an on-off switch on it, it may have been kicked to the *off* position—make sure it is *on.*

- If your hard disk is external, it has its own on-off switch that must be turned on *first* so it can boot up; then the Mac must still have its own switch turned on *also.*

- If your computer has a fan unit on top with buttons to push, those buttons still won't work unless the switch on the back of the computer is *also* on. The button on the left of the fan unit typically starts the Mac, while the button on the right will start your hard disk (but the hard disk itself should be turned on first).

- If your Mac II starts from the keyboard switch, you must make sure the switch on the back of the Mac is also on.

You're trying to start your computer and Mac just spits out your disk and/or gives you a big X. This usually happens because Mac can't find the System Folder. If you are using an external hard disk, make sure the hard disk unit itself is turned on, as well as any peripheral switches. If you are using a floppy disk, the disk you are inserting does not have a System Folder on it. Or it may have a System Folder, but the System Folder doesn't contain the System icon and/or the Finder icon. *Both* icons *must* be on the disk; and actually, both icons must be in the same folder and the folder really must be named "System Folder" or confusion may result (even on a hard disk).

The Flashing X, or The Disk Gets Spit Out

The Screen Freezes Occasionally the computer screen just up and freezes. The pointer may move around, but you can't click on anything and it doesn't respond to the keys. Most often this is the result of static electricity. You can try pressing Command–period, but it usually doesn't help. Frankly, you just have to turn the machine off. Yes, you will lose everything that hasn't been saved, which is one of the reasons you should SOS (Save Often, Stupid! . . . er, Smartie!).

Can't Find Your Document In the beginning you may very often save a document dutifully, but then when you get to your Desktop you can't find it anywhere. This is because when you saved it you weren't paying attention to which disk and/or folder you were saving it into. Be sure to read the chapter on Saving (pages 63–65, as well as 33–34), and carefully look at the dialog box pictured there so you understand how to save it into the right place.

Anyway, at the moment you can't find it. Never fear, Mr. Find File is here! Read about this guy on page 81—he'll go get your file and hand it right over to you.

When you find your file, put it in a folder you have created (page 31), just as if you were going to put it in a file folder in the filing cabinet. Press-and-drag the file icon over to the folder or disk of your choice. The folder/disk should turn *black;* when it's black, let go and the document will drop right in.

Can't Open a File Sometimes when clicking on an icon you get a message box that tells you the file is locked or in use, or maybe that an application couldn't be found.

🔒 14 items

This symbol indicates the disk is locked.

If the **disk is locked,** you'll see a little lock symbol in the upper left of the window when you open it. When a disk is locked you can't save to it, nor can you print from a locked *System* disk (if you are one of those who still works from a floppy System disk). To unlock it, first eject it. In one of the corners is a little black tab that covers or uncovers a hole. When the hole is open, the disk is locked (seems backwards, doesn't it?). So to unlock it, switch the tab back so the hole is closed. (More info on page 7.)

If the **file is locked,** click once on it and choose "Get Info" from the File menu. In the upper right corner there is a little box named "Locked" that may be checked. If it is checked, then clicking in the box will uncheck it and thus unlock the file.

If the **file is in use,** then it's in use. Usually you get this message if you try to open one of the icons that looks like a Macintosh; those are part of the System.

If it tells you **an application can't be found,** then one of two things is happening:

- The software application that the document was created in is not in the computer. Even though your document icon may *look* like SuperPaint, in order to view the document it has to go *into* the application SuperPaint to create itself.

- Some files cannot go straight from the Desktop to the application, even if the application is in the computer also. In this case, if you know the document was created in a certain application and you know that particular application is in your machine, then you must go into the *application* itself (double-click on its icon) and open the file you want from inside, choosing "Open" from the File menu.

When trying to view clip art, often you will get the message that "An application can't be found," even when the program it was generated in is on the disk. You need to open *the actual application itself,* then open each individual document through the File menu, choosing "Open" (such as MacPaint, **or** SuperPaint with the MacPaint button selected in the Open box).

Viewing Clip Art Files

If you are experiencing **system bombs** too regularly, the most common reason is that you have more than one System in your computer. One System is essential; two Systems is too many. Even though you don't see something called System Folder right there on your Desktop doesn't mean you don't have one tucked away in the depths of several other folders somewhere.

System Bombs

If you have a hard disk, don't use a floppy that also has a System on it. If the document you need is on a floppy with a System Folder, *copy the document onto your hard disk, eject the floppy, and open the document from the hard disk;* you can copy the revised file back onto the floppy when you're done.

**Find any
extra Systems**

An easy way to find all the Systems on your hard disk and on any floppy disks you are using is to ask Mr. Find File (read all about him on page 81). Move them all (except one—save the latest version!) to the Desktop and throw them in the trash. If you hold down the Option key while trashing them, you can avoid the nice dialog box that asks if you're sure you want to do this. *You won't be able to throw away the System that is booting the machine.*

Understand, though, that each System has its own collection of fonts and desk accessories. If you have customized a System Folder, save that one.

**Text Formatting
Unexpectedly
Changed**

It's not uncommon to open a file on another *System* and find major formatting changes. If you created a document on your hard disk using the font Palatino, then gave a copy of the document on disk to a co-worker who opened it up and found it had transmogrified itself into the font Helvetica, meaning all your formatting was thrown off, that's because Palatino was not in the co-worker's *System*. If the document can't find the font it was specified in, then it has to choose another from what is available. The only solution is to make sure both Systems have the same information in their System Folder and font files.

This may happen occasionally even if the fonts are the same in both Systems. Another possible reason for this is that some programs create a file in the System Folder that holds the formatting for the document. When you open up the document with a different System Folder, it can't find its formatting. If you know you are going to be taking that document to another computer, as soon as you quit creating it, go into the System Folder and find the formatting file; e.g. *Word Settings* if you are using Microsoft Word. Rename that file to correspond with the file you just created (though not exactly the same name), and put them both in the same folder.

**Printing
Doesn't Work**

• One of the most common reasons why printing won't work is because the appropriate printer icon wasn't chosen. Go to Chooser from the Apple menu and choose your printer (see pages 68 and 79).

- Make sure the printer is on, that it has paper, and that the paper tray, if there is one, is firmly attached.

- Make sure any networking cables are connected.

- On an Image Writer, make sure the Select light is on. It *must* be on in order to print.

- Also on an ImageWriter make sure the lever on the hand roller corresponds to the way you are feeding paper—that is, friction-feed for single sheets (that's the symbol with two rollers, towards the back); and pin-feed for pin-fed labels and paper (that's the symbol with one roller and little pins, pulled towards the front).

- If the disk that the *System Folder is on* has less than about 15K available, Mac cannot print. She needs some free space to send over the messages for printing. You will have to free up some space on that disk by removing a file or two.

- Sometimes gremlins prevent printing properly. If you have checked everything and there really seems to be no logical reason for it not to print, go away for a while, let someone else print to that printer, shut down, come back later, try again. This sometimes works. One never knows.

- Unusual printing problems are a common symptom of a virus attack. There is a great deal of literature available on the topic of viruses; check with your computer dealer for information and for the software available for detection and eradication. If you think you have the WDEF virus, read about rebuilding your Desktop to destroy it, page 90.

Can't Form-Feed or Line-Feed the ImageWriter Paper

If you want to form-feed or line-feed the paper, the Select light must be *off*. Be sure to turn it back on again before you try to print!

Notice that the line-feed button will feed the paper through one line at a time for four lines, then it turns into a controllable form-feed; as soon as you let go it stops. Form-feed itself will roll through an entire page length (generally 11 inches).

There's Garbage Hanging Around Outside the Trash Can

If garbage piles up around your can, it's because you didn't put it *inside* the can, but set it down *outside,* just like the kids. When the *very tip of the pointer* touches the can and turns it black, that's the time to let go. It doesn't matter if the icon itself is positioned over the can—it's the pointer tip that opens the lid.

Grey Disk Icon is Left on the Screen

A grey disk icon can mean one of two things, either it is open or it is in RAM.

Grey disk icon left on the screen after being ejected

If the disk itself is still in the floppy drive, then the grey shadow of it only means that you have already double-clicked on it and its window is open somewhere on the screen. If you can't see it because there are other windows in the way, simply double-click on the grey shadow and it will come forth as the active window.

If the disk itself is not in the floppy drive, then you most likely ejected that disk by choosing "Eject" from the File menu or by pressing Command–E. This procedure does eject the disk, but also leaves its information in Mac's *memory.* Read page 73 for a thorough explanation of what happened and how to avoid it.

Use these pages to record any new tips or shortcuts or troubleshooting techniques you happen to discover or read about.

**More of your
own tips**

INDEX

Colophon   This book was produced on a Mac SE with a 20 meg internal hard disk, Claris MacWrite II for word processing, Silicon Beach's SuperPaint for cleaning up the screen dumps, Aldus Pagemaker 3.02 for the page design and layout (thank goodness for style sheets!), an Apple Laser-Writer for proofing, and a Linotronic for final output to go to press.

The fonts are the ITC New Baskerville and the Futura families, both from Adobe Systems Incorporated.

Zapf Dingbats

In the chart to the left, find the Zapf Dingbat you wish to type. Hold down the Shift, the Option, or the Shift-and-Option keys while pressing the text character. The dingbat in the Zapf column needs no extra keys.

Text	Zapf	Shift	Option	Shift & Option
1	☜	✂	②	➚
2	☞	✠	♥	➙
3	✓	✄	♦	➜
4	✔	✂	♦	→
5	✕	☎	⑤	→
6	✖	✻	♥	➟
7	✗	©	❧	➠
8	✘	☛	♣	✿
9	✚	✈	⑥	➡
0	✎	✉	⑦	➢
-	✍	✿	⑦	⑧
=	†	☞	②	⑥
q	❑	✳	⑥	⑤
w	◗	✸	②	➢
e	✾	✜	♠	➤
r	❒	✤	♣	➥
t	▼	✳	➤	➦
y	❙	✺	⑨	➧
u	◆	✴	①	➡
i	✣	☆	✺	⇨
o	❏	✮	⑩	④
p	❐	☆	④	❸
[	✼	‘	⑨	⑩
]	✻	“	→	→
a	✿	✡	{	)
s	▲	✳	☜	⇨
d	❈	✤	❶	⇦
f	❋	◆	⑤	⇨
g	✳	✧	♦	⇨
h	✺	★	→	⇨
j	✴	✪	⑦	⇨
k	✳	☆	☞	⇨
l	●	✯	③	⇨
;	✛	✚	⑩	⊃
'	☤	✂	⑨	③
z	■	✺	⑧	➤
x	▮	✳	⑥	➘
c	✿	✜	}	(
v	❖	✱	④	↕
b	❂	✛	⑤	➤
n	■	✫	”	➤
m	○	★	⑩	➘
,	✿	✠	⑦	➤
.	✎	✝	⑧	➹
/	☍	✝	↔	①
`	✿	”	✿	→
spacebar			❶	❶
\	✳	’	⑧	⑨

n (outlined)	□
l (outlined)	○
t (outlined)	▽
s (outlined)	△
u (outlined)	◇
Opt-6 (outlined)	♡

Sh-]	"
Sh- `	"
Sh- [	'
Sh- \	'

Opt-Sh-/	①	Opt-u-space	①
Opt-1	②	Opt-=	②
Opt-l	③	Opt-Sh-'	③
Opt-v	④	Opt-Sh-o	④
Opt-f	⑤	Opt-5	⑤
Opt-x	⑥	Opt-Sh-=	⑥
Opt-j	⑦	Opt-,	⑦
Opt-\	⑧	Opt-.	⑧
Opt-Sh-\	⑨	Opt-y	⑨
Opt-;	⑩	Opt-m	⑩

Opt-d	❶	Opt-Spcbar	❶
Opt-w	❷	Opt-` *then* Sh-a	❷
Opt-Sh-p	❸	Opt-n *then* Sh-a	❸
Opt-p	❹	Opt-n *then* Sh-o	❹
Opt-b	❺	Opt-Sh-q	❺
Opt-q	❻	Opt-q	❻
Opt-0	❼	Opt--	❼
Opt-z	❽	Opt-Sh- -	❽
Opt-'	❾	Opt-[	❾
Opt-o	❿	Opt-Sh-[	❿

Here is a handy chart for finding some of the special characters available that will make your work look more professional

"	Option – [	Opening double quote
"	Option – Shift – [	Closing double quote
'	Option –]	Opening single quote
'	Option – Shift –]	Closing single quote; Apostrophe
-	Hyphen	Hyphen
–	Option – Hyphen	En dash
—	Option – Shift – Hyphen	Em dash
…	Option – ;	Ellipsis (this character cannot be separated at the end of a line as the three periods can)
•	Option – 8	Bullet
❏	o	(in font Zapf Dingbats)
■	n	(in font Zapf Dingbats)
□	n (outlined)	(in font Zapf Dingbats)
©	Option – g	Copyright symbol
™	Option – 2	Trademark symbol
®	Option – r	Registration symbol
°	Option – Shift – 8	Degree symbol: 105° F
¢	Option – $	Cents symbol
/	Option – Shift – !	Fraction bar (it doesn't descend below the base-line as the slash does)
fi	Option – Shift – 5	Ligature for **f** and **i**
fl	Option – Shift – 6	Ligature for **f** and **l**
£	Option – 3	English pound sign
¿	Option – Shift – ?	Spanish symbol
ç	Option – c	Cedilla, lowercase
Ç	Option – Shift – c	Cedilla, capital
⌘	Control – Q	(only in the Chicago font; the Control key is not on a Mac Plus keyboard)

Accent Marks

Refer to page 48 to learn how to type these in; this page is merely a quick reference

´	Option – e
`	Option – ~
¨	Option – u
~	Option – n
^	Option – i